PRAISING GOD
THROUGH THE LIVELY ARTS

PRAISING GOD
THROUGH THE
LIVELY ARTS

LINDA M. GOENS

ABINGDON PRESS
Nashville

PRAISING GOD THROUGH THE LIVELY ARTS

Copyright © 1999 by Linda M. Goens

This book is printed on acid-free paper.

Library of Congress Cataloging-in-Publication Data

Goens, Linda M., 1940-
  Praising God through the lively arts / Linda M. Goens.
    p. cm.
  Includes bibliographical references.
  ISBN 0-687-03113-3 (alk. paper)
    1. Drama in public worship.   2. Religious dance, Modern. 3. Clowns—Religious aspects—Christianity.   4. Christianity and the arts. 5. Public worship.   I. Title.
  BV289.G64   1999
  246'.7—dc21
                                                                99-17537
                                                                   CIP

All scripture quotations, unless otherwise noted, are taken from the HOLY BIBLE: NEW INTERNATIONAL VERSION®. Copyright © 1973, 1978, 1984 by the International Bible Society. Used by permission of Zondervan Publishing House. All rights reserved.

Scripture quotations marked NRSV are from the New Revised Standard Version Bible. Copyright © 1989 by the Division of Christian Education of the National Council of the Churches of Christ in the United States of America. Used by permission.

All movement hymns, songs, and prayers can be found in *The United Methodist Hymnal* (Nashville: The United Methodist Publishing House, 1989).

NOTE: Purchaser may use the activities in this book as desired as part of any service or program. Necessary photocopies of scripts and movements may be made for each presenter. There is no additional cost or fee for use by original purchaser, including the church or not-for-profit organization for which it was purchased. Use of a video or sketches for fund raising, television, radio, video, or commercial purposes is prohibited.

99 00 01 02 03 04 05 06 07 08—10 9 8 7 6 5 4 3 2 1

MANUFACTURED IN THE UNITED STATES OF AMERICA

To the presenters of the
Sonshine Company,
Scriptures Alive,
and
Spirit in Motion
who, through the sharing of their gifts,
have brought scripture to life for many;

To the pastors and members of
Church of the Saviour in Indianapolis
who opened their hearts and minds to accept
those gifts;

And to my husband, my mother, and friend Jane,
who gave me what I needed to share my gifts.

CONTENTS

FOREWORD. 9

INTRODUCTION 11

CHAPTER 1
A LEAP OF FAITH: Creating a Worship Arts
Program. 17

CHAPTER 2
EMBODYING THE SPIRIT: Drama and Scripture
Reading 29

SCRIPTURE, SKITS, AND STORIES:

THE GREAT COMMISSION: Choral Scripture Reading. . 37

*THE VINE AND THE BRANCHES: Choral Scripture
Reading.* 40

THE GOOD SHEPHERD: Scripture as Story 42

THE PARALYTIC: Scripture Skit. 45

SHOUT ALLELUIA: Contemporary Skit 49

*BRINGING UP GODLY CHILDREN: Scripture
Interpreted by Children.* 51

GOD, MY CRITIC, AND ME: Contemporary Skit 53

*A CONVERSATION WITH JESUS: Contemporary
Scripture Skit* 57

EPIPHANY: Contemporary Skit 59

GO TELL IT: Epiphany Skit 63

*PALM SUNDAY: Drama and Movement for Children
and Adults* 64

CHAPTER 3

SACRED DANCE 68
MOVEMENTS:
SPIRIT OF THE LIVING GOD: Congregational Movement
to Hymn 90
SERVICE OF THE LIGHT: Evening Meditation Service . . . 91
PSALM 104:31-35: Psalm of Praise 94
MARY/ANGEL DANCE: Advent Dance 96
SOLDIERS' DANCE: THE MOCKING OF JESUS: Good Friday
Movement 100
SYMBOLS: Good Friday Movement 106
EASTER MOVEMENT WITH RECITATION: Choreographed
Scripture Interpretation 110
PENTECOST: Scripture Interpretation with Movement . . . 114

CHAPTER 4

GOD'S MESSENGER: The Clown as Minister . . . 122
SKITS:
GIFTS IN THE SCHOOL OF LIFE: Using Our Talents . 128
THE CARPENTER: Love Thy Neighbor 134
BUILDING A CHURCH: What a Church Should Be . . . 139
SOWING SEEDS: The Parable and Its Explanation 141
TREASURES: Interpretation of Scripture 145
THE WIDOW'S MITE: Interpretation of Scripture 148

CHAPTER 5

SEASONAL SERVICES AND DRAMA SERIES . . . 151
WEEKLY DIALOGUE FOR ADVENT, INCLUDING
MUSIC, DANCE, AND A COMPLETE CHRISTMAS EVE
SERVICE 151
MAUNDY THURSDAY SERVICE: Drama with
Movement 173
GOOD FRIDAY SERVICE: The Last Words of Christ
with Monologues by Mary, the Mother of Jesus 177

APPENDIX A: Suggested Preparation Exercises and
Techniques 187
APPENDIX B: Resources and References 193
SCRIPTURE INDEX 198

FOREWORD

We need art to live fully and to grow healthy.
—Maya Angelou, *Even the Stars Look Lonesome*

P*raising God Through the Lively Arts* is a resource designed to help clergy, worship, and lay leaders energize worship services through the use of drama, movement, and clowning. The creative worship ideas presented here are readily accessible, and the methods used to implement those ideas are easily understandable. A variety of worship activities are provided, including scripture readings and adaptations, reader's theater skits (referred to as dramatic readings), sacred movement ideas, and clown skits.

The book is organized so that a church has the option of focusing on the introduction into worship of one art form at a time, such as drama and scripture reading, or beginning an arts program that regularly includes all the art forms at various times in worship. Each chapter features explanations for implementing the specific activity, such as clowning, as well as a series of ready-made scripts or movements for use in worship. In many instances scripture selections and/or hymns are suggested to accompany the activity. Physical and vocal exercises are provided in the appendixes.

This book is written for pastors and worship leaders rather than for trained theater and dance professionals, although these people will find the skits and ideas helpful for use within a church setting. Designed for those who have had little or no experience in the performing arts, the explanations presented throughout the book are easy to understand and implement with the worship activities, in many cases, requiring only one or two rehearsals.

Praising God Through the Lively Arts is unique in several ways. First, the focus here is on *doing*. The premise is to present numerous ideas for enlivening worship and other church functions, while offering specific guidance and instruction for carrying them out. *Praising God Through the Lively Arts* emphasizes taking action.

Second, the book presents material for drama, scripture reading, clowning, and liturgical dance in one resource. Moreover, although corporate worship is the primary focus here, much of the material can readily be used in educational, missional, or social settings.

Finally, another unique feature is the inward-centered nature of the presentations. These activities are not designed for "performance," but rather as expressions of worship that come from within an individual or a group. The idea here is not to perform but *to express* and *to worship*.

Finding the appropriate skits or dances to use in *Praising God Through the Lively Arts* is simple, and finding information on how to integrate presentations into worship is here as well. What isn't in this book is the courage to try something new and different. That comes from prayer. To present an activity once with less than perfect results and then to try it again demands courage too and that also comes from prayer. It's a risky path you take when including creative arts in worship, but it's also an exciting one, landscaped with spiritual mountaintops and satisfying valleys. You won't be sorry you set out on the journey.

INTRODUCTION

*God does not give us talents to make us proud.
God gives us talents so that we have something
to give to others.*
—Karen H. Whiting, *Upper Room* (May-June, 1998)

If we can create worship services that are energetic, enlightening, and forceful and that provide a continuous flow of productive activity, we will offer worship that is dynamic and contagious; and that worship brings us and keeps us closer to God. This task can be accomplished through the use of the creative arts to enhance worship services. Creative arts when used because of and for God become worship arts.

The reasons given for opposing the introduction of drama, dance, and clowning as a part of worship services are often very similar to those that once banished music: *They relate too much to the secular world,* and *they are a form of entertainment that hinders our relationship with God.* We must realize that every art form, for that matter every word spoken, can be used for good or evil, for God or man. The secret to keeping the creative arts as worship arts is in the *purpose.* We must trust ourselves to know when an art form enhances our spiritual life and when it does not; and we must believe that far from hindering our spiritual growth, the worship arts benefit all who are connected to the church.

There is a popular notion that to introduce drama, dance, or clowning into worship is to create a radically different format for worship known as "contemporary" worship, which appeals primarily to younger adults. My experience in directing a creative worship arts program for thirteen years dispels the idea that the arts and traditional worship do not mix. Traditional services are not so much changed as improved by including worship arts. It isn't a matter of replacing the sermon with drama but of including drama that illustrates an important point in the sermon. A clown skit doesn't replace scripture but delivers scripture in a more memorable manner. A dance isn't used to entertain but to set a mood for prayer. The worship arts do not function separately from the scripture and sermon message but are a means of enhancing that message.

The creative arts in worship also offer a tremendous benefit for the children and youth within the faith community. While most churches use considerable energy, time, and money to provide programs for children and youth, they often overlook them when planning worship. Often the children or youth sit idly in the sanctuary becoming familiar with the expectations and routine of worship but gaining little else. We may think, *It's nice if they receive some benefit from worship, but it is not our first priority.* Generally, the assumption is that they will get what they need spiritually in Sunday school or through the youth group. However, including a clown skit, dance, or contemporary drama in worship allows children and teenagers to get what they need within worship as well.

Another benefit is that children can be encouraged to participate in the worship arts as dancers at a very young age and then as drama presenters as they reach the appropriate age. Moreover, since the creative arts program is aimed at all church members, children and youth can participate with their parents. Scripturally based dance or drama becomes a family activity that is a new and exciting learning experience for everyone.

Let's look at specific ways worship arts benefit members of the congregation. Because their lives are busy and complex, members may arrive on Sunday morning in a state of exhaustion. Church is the first quiet, nonthreatening place they've been all week; and despite their best efforts, their attention wanders aimlessly. A few may even nod off. Those who are awake and alert often come to worship carrying heavy burdens, their minds clinging tenaciously to worries about an ill loved one or the possibility of a layoff at work or the dozen quarrelsome relatives descending on them for a holiday brunch. A good presentation of drama, dance, or clowning lures people away from their troubles almost without their realizing it.

Once their attention is engaged, it remains engaged because worship arts tend to involve people in the situations presented by making them feel emotion. They begin to fear, love, and need in conjunction with the dramatized characters and cease to be solely spectators. They begin to imagine what it is like to be a character in scripture, pondering what to do as they are caught up in the situation presented before them. Once a congregation's imagination gets into the act, literally, they *become part of the experience*, and this experience then becomes internalized as part of their own makeup. A lesson internalized is a lesson learned.

People always learn more from experience than from hearing something secondhand. Like the parables, the worship arts do not tell people what to think and how to behave but stimulate their own creative and reasoning powers, which allows them to make their own decisions about appropriate thoughts and actions.

Worship arts touch us emotionally; and when our emotions are affected, we are motivated to action, sometimes to change ourselves, sometimes to help others. If people are shown a need that kindles their feelings, they are far more likely to respond.

A short drama or movement, especially one involving

the congregation, can enhance meditation and prayer not only by creating a mood for reflection but also by giving people something to think about that helps focus their minds on God.

And finally, worship arts are extremely valuable because they appeal to a variety of personalities and learning styles. Just as teachers know that a student may learn best by visual, auditory, tactile, or kinesthetic stimulation, so a congregation member may be reached best by sermon, music, drama, clowning, or dance. Providing all forms of expression allows all people to be moved spiritually at one time or another. To ignore any of these forms is to ignore the needs of some members of a congregation.

The presenters gain as much from participating in the worship arts as do the members of the congregation who observe. In order to embody a message, it is necessary to learn the details about characters, situation, related history, and culture. It is easy to see how people who embody the scripture message will not easily forget the experience or the lesson it teaches. Whether you portray Jesus through drama, dance, or clowning, once you have taken on the character of the Savior, choosing to die in order to save the very people torturing you, you will never see the trial and crucifixion the same way again. Paul George, who played the role of Jesus in a Good Friday movement, had this to say about the experience: "I actually felt the way Jesus must have felt—humiliated, physically abused, and helpless. I have been transformed by this experience."

Another benefit to presenters of worship arts is fellowship. We could say that a group that creates together, relates together. In-depth relationships often result from the learning, sharing, and risk involved in presenting a dance, a skit, or a dramatic scripture reading.

Self-confidence is a secondary benefit of participating in the worship arts. Repeated opportunities for public speaking or dance in a safe, loving environment lead to improved performance, *increased* self-satisfaction, and sometimes further pursuit of a skill. Contributing to the overall welfare of the church lends ownership to worship services. Actively involved, presenters feel responsible for the quality of the worship service; and because they are involved and giving, they are growing spiritually.

Since this is a team project with the pastor, director, and presenters working closely to create an innovative program that brings new life to worship, mistakes are bound to occur, especially at first. A service may run too long or seem a little disjointed, but mistakes in timing can be corrected as inclusion of the arts in worship becomes more commonplace. For example, relating a passage of scripture dramatically takes no more time than reading it without inflection. While a skit may add three to ten minutes to a service, it can be balanced with a slightly shorter sermon or fewer verses from a hymn. On occasion, a dance might replace a soloist, or movement could accompany the choir's anthem.

Over time, these small but significant changes will be rewarded with expressions of gratitude such as, "The resurrection love is so wonderful! Thanks to the worship arts people for making it live."

And isn't that what we all want—to make the love of Christ live?

Chapter One

A LEAP OF FAITH
Creating a Worship Arts Program

Shoot for the moon. Even if you miss it, you will land among the stars.
—Les Brown, in Julia Cameron's *The Artist's Way*

The most essential ingredient to a worship arts program is a director, someone who selects skits and dances, organizes rehearsals, and directs presentations. Someone must be in charge, and since you are reading this book, that someone is probably you.

Wait a minute, you say. *I don't have the training or the experience to direct a worship arts program. Someone else is surely better equipped.* It's possible that among your church members there is a young, energetic, talented, experienced man or woman with a degree in dance and theater. Unfortunately, the schedules of professionals in the arts often preclude much continual active involvement in worship arts.

Well, then, you say, *I'll get the training I need, go back to school, take some classes, attend workshops, read books. When I'm ready, I'll take charge.* Now that's the right attitude! Only you will need to change the timing a bit—**Get the program started and train as you go.** If you wait until you think you are ready, it's quite possible you never will be. Remember:

Directing and participating in worship arts is an experience in *faith*. Talent and training are extremely helpful in creating a worship arts program, but they are not by any means the most essential characteristics needed in a director.

I speak from experience, having had no formal training in drama, dance, or clowning before I began experimenting with worship arts. However, I have always enjoyed all three as a spectator and as a casual participant. My journey into worship arts began with a simple folk-type dance I learned in a liturgical dance workshop. Then having seen a presentation of a short drama at another church, it occurred to me that scripture could be dramatized for a Good Friday worship service. From then on, it was a matter of learning and trying. The creative arts program outlined in this book incorporates all of the knowledge gained from all of that learning and trying.

What does a director need if not formal training? Vision. Vision and a calling. If you are in doubt, pray. Ask God if this is what you are being called to do. To have vision is to see in your mind's eye dancers praising God in worship, to hear in your mind's ear scripture readers bringing the Bible to life. In addition to a willingness to learn continually, a director should be prepared to use his or her imagination, to take risks, to persevere in the face of obstacles, and to work with others, most specifically the pastor.

Ideally, every church would have either a paid or volunteer worship arts director just as they have a choir director for music. If worship arts are to become an integral part of worship, leadership is essential. Without one person overseeing the program, it will be as successful as a choir without a director.

SIX STEPS BEFORE GETTING UNDERWAY

1. Pray. Yes, pray, once again. You, the director, feel called. Or at least you did yesterday. You visualize drama or dance or clowning or all three in worship. Or at least you did yesterday. Pray, and you will know it all again today.

2. *Talk to the Pastor.* First, you must be clear about your vision and then you must be able to illuminate that vision so vividly that others will see it also. In addition, you will need to provide an explanation of how a worship arts program can benefit both the pastor and the congregation. Re-read the introduction, which discusses the benefits of a worship arts program, or loan this book to the pastor.

3. *Seek Supporters.* Discuss your proposal with other church leaders and members as a means of generating support and excitement for the worship arts. These people, in turn, will spread the excitement on to others. Soon you will have a core of supporters who will balance out any dissenting voices. Please note that your supporters can also boost your flagging spirit when the dissenters object loudly to the program.

4. *Introduce Worship Arts to the Congregation.* Talk with your pastor to determine the best way to introduce worship arts to your congregation. How will they respond if you say nothing but simply have someone other than the pastor present a dramatic scripture reading? Should they be told beforehand that you are trying something a little different? If so, the pastor is the best person to announce that the church is going to try presenting scripture in a new way for several weeks and then evaluate the change on a specified date. This approach works well since members are given an opportunity to respond and will not feel trapped into accepting a new worship idea they may not like.

5. *Start Small.* When planning your first presentations, begin with scripture reading. For several Sundays take the scripture reading selected by the pastor and have several people read it as dialogue or in parts. Gradually move into choral scripture reading, then scripture skits, and finally contemporary message skits. Sacred movement might begin with dancers interpreting scripture or a familiar hymn with movement. Initially, do only one activity within a worship service. Later, combine dialogue scripture

reading, a dramatic skit or clowning, and a dance in one service, such as Advent, but for starters, keep it simple.

6. *Accept Mistakes and Criticism.* Do not be thwarted by criticism before or soon after starting the program. It may help to recall the reactions that Jesus received when he tried to change the way people responded to God. People are threatened by change and need time to adapt. In some cases, those most vocally opposed will not even know what sacred movement is, nor can they imagine a skit in a worship setting. Once they have an opportunity to see that everything is done as worship and not as entertainment, they will begin to relax and realize how much more dynamic worship services have become.

Mistakes, however, will be made. As with any new adventure—and this is an adventure—you will make wrong turns here and there or stumble over an obstacle. However, if you accept that blunders will occur occasionally, they won't throw you when they happen. View each mistake as an opportunity for learning and for growth.

GETTING STARTED

Seeking Presenters

To avoid connections to theater that sometimes offend people, it is a good idea to refer to *actors* and *dancers* as *presenters*; *reader's theater* as *dramatic reading*, and all performances in the worship setting as *presentations*. This change in vocabulary, may encourage those who have no training to become a part of the worship arts.

There are many ways to involve people in the program. Making a direct announcement in worship service is enough for the eager thespians. Placing a notice in the bulletin and/or newsletter will be sufficient for others. Personally ask the timid individuals you think might be interested before and after services or over the phone. Many times people have proved they possess talents hidden even from themselves. Once a young woman declined politely, indicating she was too shy and simply wasn't the type. It hadn't been two minutes since I had hung up the phone before she called back, practically yelling, "I'll do it! I want to do it!" She turned out to be one of our most expressive dancers.

Be sure to ask people repeatedly to participate after the creative arts has been instituted. Sometimes people need to see the program in action first. After they have heard several scriptures read dramatically or seen a skit performed, they may be willing to become participants.

Invite everyone to participate regardless of age or physical ability. At Church of the Saviour, several seniors in their seventies participate in the clowning and dance groups. Physical impairment does not prevent a young mother from dancing regularly. A woman who has been blind from birth is one of our most expressive presenters.

When inviting others to be a part of the creative arts, be specific. "Would you like to be in a worship drama?" is vague and threatening. Tell people exactly what you would like them to do and when. And remember that most people are open to dramatic reading, which makes this kind of presentation the best place to start in a new program.

Preparation Meetings

Rehearsals for worship arts consist of more than just practicing a dance or a script. These meetings also include prayer and scripture study, and may involve specific physical, vocal, and meditation exercises (see appendix A). Listed below is a basic format that works well in keeping the focus of each meeting on worship and self-improvement.

— BASIC MEETING FORMAT —

1. *Planning and purpose*. At the first meeting, outline what presentation is to be done and when. Subsequent meetings may discuss problems, costuming, or other details here.
2. *Sharing*. Share concerns. (Note: Allowing each person to share as part of prayer is one way to help people keep their remarks brief.)
3. *Centering*. Connect with the spirit within. Meditation music is helpful for some people, as is dim lighting and a glowing candle.
4. *Prayer*. Connect with God. Ask the Holy Spirit to touch your spirit; to inspire you creatively; to reduce worries, fears, and inhibitions—all of which place obstacles in the channel between you and God.
5. *Warm-ups*. Physical and vocal exercising (see appendix A).
6. *Rehearse*.
7. *Close with prayer*.

COSTUMING, MAKEUP, AND LIGHTING

Costuming, makeup, lighting, and props can and must be kept at a minimum. See specific chapters on drama, dance, and clowning for costuming ideas; but in general avoid anything expensive and elaborate. The lighting provided for worship services should be sufficient for most presentations. Both drama and dance can be enhanced by raising and lowering lights at appropriate times, but this isn't absolutely necessary. Props are seldom used except during clowning skits.

Each director will need to establish guidelines concerning letting others see costuming before and after presentations. I believe that on most occasions, presenters should be able to dress for their presentations and join the congregation in worship since they are not performing a show for an audience but worshiping with a congregation. If it is preferred that presenters stay out of sight when costumed, they will miss most of worship, which is neither fair nor spiritually beneficial to them. On the other hand, since a clown sitting in the congregation may be distracting, especially for children, our clown presenters usually remain out of sight until time for their skit. Afterward, they join the congregation dressed in street clothes. This is one of the benefits of keeping makeup simple. A funny hat, jacket, and two red dots can be removed quickly. Full makeup and costume would take until well after the service is over to remove.

ENLIST THE HELP OF OTHERS

If special music is needed as background for a drama or dance, contact an instrumentalist, the choir director, or a vocalist early in the planning process. For dance rehearsals, you will need an audio recording of the music as soon as possible. If a recording of the actual choir singing is not available, then at least the musical background can be used.

When introducing your worship arts program to the congregation, announce the need for seamstresses and carpenters. Let these artists know well in advance when you need certain props or costumes.

A STEP-BY-STEP DIRECTOR PLAN

1. *Meet with the pastor.* Discuss the scripture and theme for the coming weeks or months, sharing what you and he or she would like to see incorporated in worship and planning as far in advance as possible.

2. *Select worship arts activities.* Decide what type of drama, movement, or clowning is most appropriate for each Sunday and how soon rehearsing needs to begin for each. If a script has to be ordered, consider the time neces-

sary before its arrival. Also, consider how much time you will need for choreographing or writing your own choral scriptures or skits.

3. *Make copies of scripts.* Leave one with the pastor. If there is no script, write out a description of what is to be included in the presentation and the service. Hint: scriptures copied from the Bible can be enlarged for easier reading.

4. *Meet with the pastor again.* Confirm the activities and schedule you have planned and revise as needed. Sometimes a worship service theme can be changed to a more distant Sunday to allow for rehearsal time. Sometimes scripture can be changed so that it is more conducive to a skit yet still exemplifies the same theme. Listen to ideas that could improve any given skit or dance, and when necessary, seek help with understanding a scripture or theme before beginning rehearsals.

5. *Mark a rehearsal schedule on your calendar.* Consider the following: Dances require about one and one-half hours of rehearsal time per verse of a hymn, for example. Short dramatic readings can be prepared in one rehearsal. Memorized pieces and clown skits may require two or three rehearsals, depending on how complicated or lengthy they are.

6. *Purchase 3-ring folders and insert scripts.* Presenters can then make notes during rehearsal or highlight their parts without marring their Bibles. Furthermore, folders are more attractive than loose sheets of paper and are easier to handle.

7. *Begin rehearsals.* If you do not meet with a group regularly, announce the first meeting a couple of weeks in advance and discuss other needed rehearsals at that time.

8. *Confirm worship plans with the pastor.* Before special worship services such as Easter, meet with the pastor again to confirm presentation and order of service. Other services can be discussed over the phone.

9. *Meet regularly with the pastor.* If the worship arts become a regular feature of Sunday worship services, weekly or

biweekly meetings provide an opportunity to evaluate the program in general, to discuss challenges that present themselves along the way, and to share spiritual insights.

10. *Meet with presenters before worship services.* Set a time and place to assemble immediately before a worship service in which drama or movement is to be presented. Spend a few moments in prayer together and check for last-minute changes in the bulletin or program. Clarify once again when, where, and how people enter and exit. Run through dances and skits, even if it's just going through the motions in a small room.

11. *Praise and evaluate.* Immediately after the worship service, locate, thank, and commend each presenter. When a participant feels bad about an error made during the presentation, it's important to listen and empathize. Avoid minimizing a person's feelings by insisting, "You did fine." Or "Don't worry about it." Or "No one noticed." It's better to let the person know you've experienced the same feeling when you've made mistakes. One of the most helpful mistakes I ever made was to turn the wrong way at the climactic end of a celebration dance to run smack into another dancer. We smiled and hugged each other and went on, but I was mortified, not only to have made a mistake but to have interfered with another dancer. Later, several people commented that my mistake proved to them that our dancing was a worship experience, not a performance.

It is also important to regularly evaluate your presentations, if not right after the service, at the next meeting. Encourage participants to critique their own presentation. Often they are better able to accept criticism when it comes from another presenter. Often, even novice presenters will recognize the need for improvement. This is teamwork. In this respect, the director acts more as a facilitator and participant than boss.

12. *Use the sanctuary creatively.* Be creative in placing dramatists and dancers, even scripture readers, using the structure of your sanctuary to its fullest. If permitted, use

aisles, balconies, even choir lofts. Since this is not a performance on a stage, it is not necessary for presenters to always dance facing the congregation, nor are readers required to sit on stools in nice straight lines. As long as participants can be seen and heard, they should not be confined to one small area of presentation. Visually pleasing groupings add interest.

ADDITIONAL HELPS FOR THE DIRECTOR

Expect the Best from Children

Select activities for children that correspond to their capabilities. For example, a child under seven years will generally not be able to present anything but the simplest movements or dramas. One good way to involve younger children is to provide them with a leader who is an older child or youth; the younger each child, the more leaders will be needed for them to follow.

It is true that children are cute no matter what they do in a worship service, and the congregation will love them because they are their children. However, children can be both cute and capable. They simply need plenty of undistracted rehearsal time, lots of instruction, guidance, praise, and even more repetition. Hold rehearsals in the sanctuary whenever possible. It is important for them to enter, exit, and move during the rehearsal as they will in the presentation.

Teach little ones to respect the sanctuary. While they should be permitted to talk and move around, remind them that running, roughhousing, and screaming are not appropriate behavior.

Expect the Best from Presenters

What is true for children is also true for youth and adults. It is not un-Christian to encourage your participants to work hard and give their best. Give people plenty of suggestions and practice, and they will reward you. Of course, most presentations in the church setting will not be professional, but being professional is not the goal—communication is.

However, there is a fine line between expecting the best from participants and demanding perfection. This is a spiritual enterprise, not a theatrical performance; and while we always have to remember that the better our presentation, the more effective our sharing of the gospel, demanding professional quality from people unequipped to give it will take the joy out of the activity, which, of course, defeats the purpose of having creative art in worship in the first place.

Keep It Light

Including creative arts in worship on a regular basis is work, yet it is also the most fun you are ever going to have—if you keep it light. Have fun, let the participants have fun, don't be afraid to laugh at your own mistakes, and don't be afraid of foolishness. Participants will cut up and joke around occasionally during rehearsal even when they are rehearsing serious scripture. It helps to remember that surely Jesus had a sense of humor, considering how he used sometimes absurd analogies when making a very serious point. Laughter lessens tension and loosens us up to be better communicators of our message.

Also, remember to be flexible if something isn't working. If your dramatists cannot say a phrase without stumbling over the words and it's not actual scripture reading, change the phrase. A difficult scripture reading can sometimes be improved by using a different Bible version or by referring to another Gospel for the same story. Portions of a script can be dropped for various reasons. Dance steps can be simplified when necessary. Let your presenters help. Listen to their ideas and implement some of them. This builds their confidence while helping you.

BASIC REQUIREMENTS FOR BEGINNING A WORSHIP ARTS PROGRAM

1. A creative arts program must have a director.
2. Enlist the support of the pastor.
3. Commit yourself to programming creative arts in worship for at least a year before evaluating its effectiveness in enlivening worship.
4. Find people to support the program and encourage them to promote it with enthusiasm.
5. Look to your supporters for energy when yours is flagging.
6. Start small and simple, expecting the best your presenters can do, but include either dance, drama, or clowning in services regularly.
7. Attend workshops and classes.
8. Remember that criticism is to be expected and acknowledged but shouldn't defeat your purpose.
9. Mistakes are always learning experiences.
10. Keep prayer a regular part of the program.

BE PREPARED

You're on your way! Congratulations for taking this innovative step! But be prepared! Be prepared for spiritual growth you never imagined, for making close friends, for learning what it's like to create engaging worship services each week, and for developing creative skills you didn't know you had. But most important, be prepared for JOY.

Chapter Two

EMBODYING THE SPIRIT
Drama and Scripture Reading

Worship that is life-giving, worship that is a real response to God's grace, tells the good news in the present tense.

—Ann Weems, *Reaching for Rainbows*

Fascinating, absorbing, revealing—scripture delivered as the drama it so often is takes people by surprise. Drama in worship may include short memorized plays or skits, but expressive readings of scripture or message skits constitute drama as well and are the focus of this chapter. The simple act of reading becomes drama when participants *embody* the characters, speaking from within rather than simply reading *about* the characters. Through voice, facial expression, posture, and an occasional gesture, presenters encourage the congregation to see set, action, and costumes in their imaginations.

With dramatic reading, whether scripture or skit, no sets, props, costumes, or special lighting is required. No blocking or memorization means fewer rehearsals and less anxiety that often keeps presenters from concentrating on characterization and on what the literature is trying to convey.

CONCERNS ABOUT ACCURACY

Pastors often share the following concerns about accuracy when presenting scripture in a dramatic way. Should scripture be delivered word for word from the Bible in every circumstance, or can wording be changed for better understanding or repeated for emphasis? Can the words *he said* be deleted in a dialogue reading? Is it all right to substitute wording from another Bible version because it is more understandable or dramatic? What about adding a sentence or two when telling scripture as story?

To be bound absolutely to word-for-word reproductions from any given translation can be restrictive and limiting in a dramatic presentation, sometimes placing an obstacle in the way of insight and creativity. On the other hand, many people do not know scripture very well and will be inclined to believe that every word spoken *about* the Bible is *from* the Bible.

The answer to the problem, then, is clear. When a dramatic presentation is not a word-for-word recitation of scripture, indicate this to the congregation by placing qualifiers in the bulletin with phrases such as "an interpretation," "based on," or "a story from. . . ." The pastor may want to reiterate this point verbally, encouraging the congregation to read the day's scripture later at home. One or two verses from the day's presentation may be included within the sermon for emphasis.

PREPARATION MEETINGS

As indicated in chapter 1, all preparation meetings should begin with centering time and prayer as well as warm-up exercises (see appendix A for specific directions on centering and warm up). At the first meeting, presenters should be given basic information about the drama—whether it is a simple scripture reading, clown skit, or memorized drama and the date of presentation. If there are more presenters at the meeting than parts in the drama, the extras may be given parts in the next worship drama that is listed on the schedule and/or be encouraged to participate in discussion and to listen and evaluate rehearsals of the piece.

The first practice of a piece will begin with a read-through followed by discussion of the plot, characters, and message. This is an excellent way to study the Bible, since in order to know how to speak as a character, a presenter must understand the circumstances from which that character is speaking and what his or her motivation and emotional makeup must have been at the time. Remember there is seldom only one way to speak a line. For example, interpretations of Judas have ranged from his being the devil incarnate to a philanthropist who, in his zeal to help the poor, betrayed a friend. Obviously, a devilish Judas will speak with different intonation and expression than a misguided benevolent Judas.

Further read-throughs will concentrate on diction, expression, and pacing. Enunciation, inflection, and projection should be emphasized. Listen for clear pronunciation of consonants since we all tend to slur and drop consonants, a habit that hinders understanding for audiences in a sanctuary.

Insist, also, that participants speak slowly, pausing between sentences, and pausing for longer periods after critical moments. It is okay to stop talking and to swallow. Moments of silence after a momentous verse in scripture allow the congregation reflection time and add drama to the reading. Remember also that most people speak faster before an audience than in rehearsal. Remind presenters of this often.

A final rehearsal should take place in the sanctuary so that there is no confusion about entrances, exits, and places of delivery. Those not actually presenting in a particular piece should take seats in various places in the sanctuary. Presenters should be encouraged to speak directly to those people. The temporary audience can then evaluate loudness and clarity.

Children are perfectly capable of speaking loudly enough to be heard. Just listen to them when you most want them to be quiet. Make a game of line repetition by having them start in a whisper and end in a shout. Stand outside the sanctuary, telling them you want to hear every word clearly.

Emphasize good posture. Slumped shoulders, lowered heads, and garbled voices direct sound to the floor where only crawling things will hear. In contrast, erect posture communicates confidence, which commands the audience's attention. Unless there is a specific reason for slouching or hanging the head, such as character depiction, presenters should sit or stand with straight backs, shoulders down, and chins parallel to the floor.

Both adults and children should approach their place of delivery with a confident stride and composed demeanor. Exits should be accomplished in the same way. Remind participants to remain in place for one or two seconds after the conclusion of a piece to avoid the appearance of relieved flight.

PLACEMENT OF PRESENTERS

Consider using stools for readers of skits longer than a couple of minutes since they are high enough for presenters to be seen from the back of the sanctuary and they prevent long periods of standing. However, readers may also stand, kneel, or sit (if they are on steps or risers where they can be seen). All presenters in a skit or scripture reading do not have to do the same thing. For instance, the person reading the words of Jesus might be sitting, with those reading the disciples' parts kneeling at Jesus' feet while those reading the parts of the Pharisees stand a little distance away.

Grouping characters, even if they are reading, helps dramatize a situation. For example, before they approach to ask their questions, James and John might huddle together as if discussing their place in heaven while Jesus looks on from several feet away (Mark 10:35). Or the Pharisees, debating strategy, may be grouped in one place while Jesus speaks from someplace else, even if it is only a few feet in front, back, or to the side (Matthew 26:1-5).

If a presenter has no further lines but the drama is not complete, he or she may (1) freeze in position, (2) drop the head and freeze, (3) turn around and face the back, or (4) exit.

PROPS, LIGHTING, AND COSTUMES

Memorized skits or plays may require more in the way of set and props than dramatic reading, but carefully selected plays can be presented with a minimum of set and props, or with none at all. If special lighting is necessary, check the yellow pages for theatrical companies that rent lighting equipment, or consult a do-it-yourselfer for inexpensive ideas. For example, spotlights and floods can be purchased from the hardware store, painted black, mounted on poles, and attached to the pews. Candles and lanterns can also be used to provide lighting when mood is important, and sometimes can even add sufficient light to read a script.

As for costuming, most often drama presenters will be in street clothes; occasionally they may wear more uniform clothing, for example, all performers wearing black turtle-necks when doing a Good Friday reading. Patterns for biblical costumes are easy to find, and the robes and head-dresses can be saved and used over and over. Unless you have a huge church or the drama is a full play with direct lighting, there is no special makeup required or desired.

WAYS TO PRESENT SCRIPTURE

Part Reading

Part reading is simply two or more presenters reading a designated number of verses. Sometimes part reading can be done in a conversational manner, as if two people are telling a story together the way we might share an experience at a family gathering, a sort of here's-what-happened-no-let-me-tell-it approach. Regardless of how it's read, just having more than one voice commands attention.

Dialogue

Dialogue reading requires a reader for each character speaking, as designated by quotation marks, as well as a narrator. If there are numerous characters such as in the trial scenes on Good Friday, bit parts like the soldiers and the crowd can be read by the same reader. Unless needed for clarification, references to who is speaking should be deleted. Dramatic readers must match facial expression and posture with voice tone. They may look occasionally at each other, directly at the audience, at some distant place above the heads of the audience, or heavenward.

While dramatic readers are not expected to memorize their material, they should be thoroughly familiar with it and be able to recite a phrase or two by heart, looking at the audience for emphasis.

Choral Scripture Reading

A choral presentation is done by a group of presenters reading in unison, sometimes broken up by a solo reading or another combination of readers—all men, followed by all women, followed by a solo, then everyone, and so forth. A choral reading may consist of a scripture selection read directly from the Bible in chorus. Or a director may want to emphasize certain verses by having them repeated by a chorus while the rest of the scripture is read solo. Another approach to choral reading consists of a chorus summarizing or rephrasing several phrases read by one or two readers. Any method of choral reading is beneficial for dramatizing scripture. Its rhythm and repetition hold the attention of listeners and help them remember the scripture later. For the presenters choral reading takes considerable practice, but it is great fun.

In the beginning it is advisable to keep choral readers to a small number. The more people reading in chorus, the harder it is to read in unison and the more difficult for the congregation to understand the words and appreciate this type of reading. Start with three or four readers in chorus, increasing the number later.

Choral presenters may stand together as does a musical choir with the solo readers stepping forward to read, then stepping back when finished. Small groups of readers may also take their places at opposite ends of the sanctuary, in the balcony, or in any other interesting arrangement.

There are three major concerns with choral reading that take special practice: beginning together with confidence, pacing, and inflection. The group needs to begin speaking in perfect unison, to pause together at punctuation and other designated points, and to speak with the same inflection (for example, loudly, softly, harshly, tenderly), emphasizing the same words in the same way, and so on. The exception to this occurs where scripture calls for groups of people responding together as in a crowd. Obviously, the mob that yelled "Crucify him!" didn't speak exactly in unison with the same inflection.

Choral readers may have a director as a choir does to help them speak as a chorus, or they may have among them a designated leader to watch.

Skits

Worship skits may embellish scripture by adding dialogue for characters present in a Bible story or through personalizing bystanders by giving them names and dialogue. They may be contemporary adaptations of scripture, or they may illustrate a theme. The aim of a worship skit is to provide knowledge and understanding of the Bible, much like Bible study. The skit attempts to answer such questions as, What were people in the story thinking, Why did they do what they did? and How does the message relate to us today?

In addition to using the bulletin to identify when scripture has been adapted or revised, it is also sometimes helpful to give background information for presentations, such as setting, character identification, and time.

Storytelling

When storytelling, the presenter memorizes a scripture passage or other material and speaks directly to the congregation in a casual, warm, conversational manner, making eye contact as often as possible. When speaking dialogue, the storyteller changes the inflection of his or her voice to match that of the character and changes the direction of his focus, as well. Biblical storyteller Dennis Dewey suggests that you visualize the story, placing a given character in a specific place near you, then speak *from* that place when you are the character assigned to that space and speak *to* that space when you speak to that character.

Storytelling is a marvelous way for a congregation to hear of a biblical event in a more personal way, which often allows them to hear it as if for the first time. Telling the story of Moses each week as a summer series or recounting the traditional Christmas stories each Sunday in Advent allows people to identify details they have missed before, as well as to relate much more clearly to the emotional responses of the characters. Members of the congregation have often mentioned how they look forward to the next Sunday's presentation when we have presented scripture in a series.

Two or more storytellers presenting scripture and related material can be equally as effective, and it lessens the amount of material one person needs to memorize. Another method of storytelling is to have one person relate the scripture as story while another person tells a story about a related subject. (See "The Good Shepherd" on page 42.)

Interaction with the audience through eye contact is vital in storytelling. Gestures and movement may be vigorous, minimal, or nonexistent with only facial expressions and the voice used to convey the story. Each storyteller has a style that is as natural to him or her as his or her conversational style. Unless the storyteller is professionally trained, it is best to allow the story to be told in the person's natural speaking style, but don't be afraid to suggest alteration of pacing and volume to improve delivery.

SCRIPTURE, SKITS, AND STORIES

All presentations, including scripture, may be memorized. If reading, presenters should be very familiar with the material.

Estimate approximately one minute per page as the length of time required for any given skit.

THE GREAT COMMISSION

Choral Scripture Reading

SCRIPTURE: Matthew 28:16-20
THEME: Evangelism/Witnessing
PRESENTERS: Reader One, Jesus, any number for chorus.

PRESENTATION

Reader 1: The eleven disciples went to Galilee to the mountain where Jesus had told them to go. When they saw Jesus, they worshiped him; but some doubted. Then Jesus came to them and said:

Jesus: All authority in heaven and on earth has been given to me.

Chorus: Jesus has the authority.

Jesus: Therefore go and make disciples of all nations, baptizing

Chorus: Baptizing

Jesus: In the name of the Father

Chorus: The Father

Jesus: And of the Son

Chorus: The Son

Jesus: And of the Holy Spirit.

Chorus: The Holy Spirit.

Jesus: Teach them to obey everything I have commanded you.

Chorus: And teach them—wait—what has he commanded?

Reader 1: He spent his life teaching. You remember.

Chorus: You tell us.

Reader 1: First, love God above everything.

Chorus: Love God.

Reader 1: Above everything.

Chorus: Above everything.

Reader 1: Love and take care of each other, even the unlovable ones.

Chorus A: The dirty?

Chorus B: And the smelly?

Chorus C: And the undeserving ones?

Reader 1: Yes, unless you are perfect, do not judge who is good and who is bad.

Chorus: Do not judge.

Reader 1: Love each other.

Chorus: Love each other.

Reader 1: Forgive each other.

Chorus: Forgive each other.

Reader 1: Now you remember: Go and teach all nations everything Jesus commanded.

Chorus A: I don't think we're qualified...

Chorus B: Or good enough...

Chorus C: Or smart enough.

Reader 1: Don't worry. You won't be alone. Remember what Jesus told you.

Jesus: Surely I am with you always, to the very end of the age.

Reader 1: Jesus is with you always . . .

Chorus: To the end of the age. To the end of the age.

THE VINE AND THE BRANCHES

Choral Scripture Reading

SCRIPTURE: John 15:1-6, 9-12
THEME: The connections between us and Jesus and Jesus and God help create the love and fruitfulness of our love and faith.
PRESENTERS: Two readers and any number for chorus.

PRESENTATION

Reader 1: I am the true vine and my Father is the gardener.

Reader 2: Jesus was an outgrowth of God.

Chorus: Because of God.

Reader 1: He cuts off every branch in me that bears no fruit, while every branch that does bear fruit, he prunes so that it will be even more fruitful.

Reader 2: Jesus grew in perfection under the tender care of God.

Chorus: Because of God.

Reader 1: You are already clean because of the word I have spoken to you. Remain in me, and I will remain in you. No branch can bear fruit by itself; it must remain in the vine. Neither can you bear fruit unless you remain in me.

Reader 2: Jesus and his followers must stay connected to be fruitful.

Chorus: The connection is in the word.

Reader 1: I am the vine; you are the branches.

Chorus: I am the vine; *you* are the branches. *(Point to congregation.)*

Reader 1: If a man remains in me and I in him, he will bear much fruit; apart from me you can do nothing.

Reader 2: We must stay connected to the Christ.

Chorus: We must stay connected to the Christ.

Reader 1: If anyone does not remain in me, he is like a branch that is thrown away and withers; such branches are picked up, thrown into the fire, and burned.

Reader 2: If we do not remain connected to Christ, we will wither.

Chorus: Withered, we will die.

Reader 1: As the Father has loved me, so have I loved you.

Reader 2: God loves Jesus. In turn, Jesus loves us.

Chorus: He loves us.

Reader 1: Now remain in my love. If you obey my commands, you will remain in my love, just as I have obeyed my Father's commands and remain in his love.

Reader 2: If you love him, you will try to please him.

Chorus: We can try. We can always try.

Reader 1: I have told you this so that my joy may be in you and that your joy may be complete.

Chorus and **Reader 2:** To love God is to know joy.

Reader 1: My command is this: Love each other as I have loved you.

Reader 2: It is a circle of love. God loved Jesus, Jesus loves us, we are to love each other; and as we love each other, we are loving God.

Chorus: A circle of love.

Reader 2: The gardener, the vine, the branches.

Chorus: We are connected.

THE GOOD SHEPHERD

Scripture as Story
(Based on information from *Jesus and His Times* [Reader's Digest General Books, 1973] and *Harper's Bible Dictionary* [Harper&Row, 1973].)

SCRIPTURE: John 10:1-18 *(The story is based on this passage and should be memorized, or nearly-so, for storytelling.)*

THEME: Jesus cares for and protects us if we know his voice and follow him.

PRESENTERS: One to three; the story is set up for three tellers but may be combined and told by one or two.

PRESENTATION

Storyteller 1: Sheep. Let's look at sheep through the eyes of the Palestinian some 2000 years ago. Sheep provided food, milk, wool for weaving and even wearing, and covering for tents. Sheep were a medium of exchange and were used as offerings for religious sacrifices. Therefore, this furry creature figured in every single vital aspect of life: food, clothing, shelter, business, and religion.

Storyteller 2: We, a sophisticated urban people, think of these animals rather romantically. We think sheep are lovable, passive, and defenseless. People of biblical days considered their sheep to be lovable, passive, and defenseless. Nice to know we are right about something.

Storyteller 3: The shepherd had a very hard job. He worked and slept outdoors in the rain and wind and beneath a hot sun. He ate only what he could carry. He didn't drive his sheep before him, but led them—to good grazing land, to water, to shelter. If one fell into a rocky crevice, the shepherd had to climb down to retrieve it or pull it to safety with his staff. An injured sheep had to be carried. A shepherd had to be agile and strong. And the shepherd worked alone. All the time—alone. Except for the sheep. And do you know? The shepherd wasn't very well respected in those days.

Storyteller 2: Bet you think they are all alike, those sheep. If-you've-seen-one, you've-seen-them-all kind of thing? Right? Wrong. A shepherd of a small flock could tell one sheep from another; sometimes he even gave them names. Calling them, "Here, Martha." "Come, Harold." And the sheep responded, not because they knew their own names, but because they knew the shepherd's voice.

Storyteller 1: To protect the sheep, the shepherd built a sheepfold. This was an enclosure with high stone walls but no gate. There was no need. The shepherd, himself, provided the gate, lying down across the opening to the sheepfold so that he would know when a sheep tried to wander away and when anything dangerous tried to enter.

Storyteller 2: And many dangers threatened the sheep: bears, leopards, and jackals, for instance. A shepherd could die trying to defend his charges.

Storyteller 3: Thieves sometimes scaled the stone walls. They would sneak off with sheep in the crooks of their arms, for the sheep would not follow willingly.

Storyteller 2: They only followed the one they trusted.

Storyteller 1: Jesus told a story about sheep and their shepherd. He pointed out that a man who enters a sheepfold other than through the door is a thief. He said that the sheep will not follow such a man willingly because they don't know him. The shepherd enters by the door, calls his sheep by name, and leads them out and away. They follow because they know his voice.

Storyteller 2: The disciples didn't get it. Of course. They hardly ever did, you know, not on the first try. Jesus either had to tell the story another way or explain what he meant. They understood about the sheep and shepherd all right, but they knew Jesus wasn't really talking about sheep and shepherds. He never seemed to be talking about *(pause)* well, what he was talking about.

Storyteller 3: Jesus explained: A thief comes to harm, but I come to do good. I will lay down my life to protect you. I will not leave you when danger comes the way the hired man leaves the sheep when the wolf comes. I know you, my people, and you know me; you know my voice. I will not leave you in the care of a hired man, and you will not follow a stranger whose voice you do not know. I have taken the job of shepherd of my own free will. If necessary, I lay down my life of my own free will. I have been given this job by God, my father.

Storyteller 1:   And so it is with a shepherd and his sheep.

Storyteller 2:   And so it is with Jesus and his people.

THE PARALYTIC

Scripture Skit

SCRIPTURE: Mark 2:1-12
THEME: Helping bring those in need to Christ requires perseverance and resourcefulness. Scripture reveals Jesus' authority to forgive sins.
PRESENTERS: Six to eight; friends can double as teachers of the Law.

PRESENTATION

Narrator: *(Recite more or less from memory)* Scripture doesn't tell us what the four friends you are about to meet said to each other on the day of their friend's healing, but we can imagine it might have gone like this. Listen to a familiar story.

(Pause and continue reciting or reading.) A few days after healing a man with leprosy, when Jesus again entered Capernaum, the people heard that he had come home. So many gathered that there was no room left, not even outside the door; and he preached the word to them. Some men came, bringing to him a friend who was paralyzed, carried by four of them.

Friend 1: Look at that crowd! We can't even see the door, much less get through it.

Friend 2: I can't believe it! Jesus is always surrounded by people; but I thought if we came this early, we would be able to . . .

Friend 3: I told you this would happen, didn't I? Didn't I tell you?

Friend 4: All right. All right, you told us. The question is now, How do we get him inside?

Friend 2: You two could push through the crowd, making a pathway; and we two can follow carrying him.

Friend 3: *(sarcastically)* Oh, sure. Great idea.

Friend 2: I don't see a thing wrong with it.

Friend 1: None of us is strong enough to push through that many people. Look how they are all jammed together. I'm not sure they could move if they wanted to.

Friend 3: *(sarcastic)* Which they probably don't.

Friend 4: *(thinking)* If we could get him to the roof—yes, that's it. We'll take him up to the roof.

Friend 3: The roof? You're crazy.

Friend 4: No, really. We take him to the ladder around back where there are no people, and one of us carries him over his shoulders up the ladder. We make a hole and lower him down.

Friend 1: You think it will work?

Friend 2: We won't know until we try.

Friend 3: We'll be the laughingstock of the whole town if it doesn't; *(hesitates)* but if he is to be cured, we must get him to Jesus somehow. So—all right, let's try it.

Narrator: They made an opening in the roof above Jesus, and, after digging through it, lowered the mat their friend was lying on. When Jesus saw their faith, he spoke to the man who was paralyzed.

Jesus: Son, your sins are forgiven.

Narrator: Some Pharisees standing nearby were appalled at this statement; and though they did not speak, their thoughts condemned Jesus.

Pharisee 1: Why does this man talk like that? Saying your sins are forgiven?

Pharisee 2: How dare this man dishonor God in this way! *(Or)* This man is blaspheming. *(Or both lines could be said.)*

Pharisee 1: Only God can forgive sins.

Pharisee 2: Who does this Jesus think he is, forgiving a man's sins as if he were God?

Jesus: Why are you thinking these things? Which is easier: to say to the man who is paralyzed, "Your sins are forgiven," or to say, "Get up, take your mat and walk"? It is necessary that you know the Son of Man has authority on earth to forgive sins.

Narrator: With this statement, Jesus turned deliberately from the **Pharisees** and spoke with great authority to the man who was paralyzed.

Jesus: I tell you—get up! Take your mat and go home!

Narrator: He got up, took his mat, and walked out in full view of them all. This amazed everyone, and they praised God, saying, "We have never seen anything like this."

(**Variation:** *Instead of the* **Narrator's** *last sentence, the speakers could speak almost simultaneously, as they would in such a circumstance.*)

Friend 1: Praise God!

Friend 2: I've never seen anything like this before!

Friend 3: Amazing!

Friend 4: I can hardly believe it!

Narrator: And so it was that the man who was paralyzed came to be cured.

SHOUT ALLELUIA

Contemporary Skit

SCRIPTURE: Matthew 25:31-40
THEME: Care for others and you will see Christ.
PRESENTERS: Three—an enthusiastic, childlike witness; a
   skeptic; a parent-teacher figure.
DIRECTOR'S NOTE: *This skit can be memorized or read; however, readers should be so familiar with the script that they
   hardly need to look at it.*

PRESENTATION

Reader 1: I met Jesus last night!

Reader 2: You mean his spirit. You felt his spirit.

Reader 1: No! I mean I met Jesus.

Reader 3: Really. A lot of people would like to know
what Jesus looks like. Tell us.

Reader 1: Well, he was blind and nearly deaf, and he
didn't have any teeth, and one of his feet was
blackened from gangrene.

Reader 2: It sounds like one of those he helped, not like
Jesus himself.

Reader 1: It was him, I tell you. Want to know how I
found out?

Reader 3: Something tells me we're going to find out
about it whether we want to know or not.

Reader 2: Let her [him] talk. Can't you see she [he]
needs to talk?

Reader 3: So talk.

Reader 1: Here's what happened. One of the protective
boots slipped off the damaged foot and the

blankets just touching his flesh hurt him. His foot smelled really bad and looked terrible, sickening, actually; but I had to do something. None of the nurses had been in for ages, and he was suffering. There was no one else. So, I fixed the boot in place, and suddenly—well, I knew it was Jesus.

Reader 3: So, how does a person feel the day after touching the foot of Jesus?

Reader 1: Good! I feel really good! I'd like to shout with the joy of how good I feel!

Reader 2: Well, you can't. You're in church.

Reader 1: I could dance with the joy. Just jump right up and dance!

Reader 3: You can't dance, either. Not just like that, so sudden and unplanned.

Reader 1: Sing, then?

Reader 2: It's okay to sing, but . . .

Reader 1: *(bursts into joyful song such as "Joy to the World" or "I've Got the Joy")*

Reader 3: *(interrupting quickly)* Not now! What's the matter with you?

Reader 1: It's the joy. I just wanted to sing with the joy of knowing Jesus. Besides, she [he] said I could.

Reader 2: You have to wait for the right time. When all of them sing.

Reader 1: *(disappointed)* Oh. Okay, I'll wait, but it's hard when you feel so full of spirit. You want to shout "Alleluia," you know?

Reader 2: I know, but you have to remember—

Reader 3: There's a time and a place for shouting "Alleluia."

Reader 2: You have to wait until everyone else does.

Reader 1: Maybe everyone wants to now.

Reader 2: Now?

Reader 1: Sure. Shout "Alleluia" everybody!

Reader 1: *(steps forward and gestures to congregation as* **2** *and* **3** *join her [him] in shouting with the congregation)* Alleluia!

(If the congregation does not join in, **Reader 1** *should gesture to them again and repeat the last line until they do.)*

BRINGING UP GODLY CHILDREN

Scripture Interpreted by Children

SCRIPTURE: Matthew 7:9-12, 19:13-14; Proverbs 22:6

THEME: Don't hinder the children from coming to Christ. Teach a child to do unto others as would be done unto him or her. Bring up a child in the way he or she should go, and he or she won't depart from it.

PRESENTERS: Two children or youth, One adult to read scripture at the end. **Child 1** speaks with happiness in the voice, smiles, and appears open and confident, may be dressed in cheerful colors, bows in hair, and so forth. **Child 2** does not smile, speaks with force and with anger or bitterness, may be dressed in darker colors, may be slightly unkempt.

DIRECTOR'S NOTE: *Skit may be read, but memorized is preferred.*

PRESENTATION

Child 1: When I asked for bread, you gave me bread, warm and fresh from the oven. Thank you.

Child 2: When I asked for fish, you said—I'm too tired to cook fish. I learned not to ask for anything.

Child 1: We went to the fair, and you held my hand so I wouldn't get lost. Thank you for protecting me.

Child 2: We went to the park and you said, "Go find something to do for a while." I learned I'm not wanted.

Child 1: One morning I woke up with a sore throat. You took me to the doctor right away. Thank you for worrying about me.

Child 2: One morning I woke with a stomachache. You said, "It can't be that bad. You're going to school." I learned nobody believes me.

Child 1: I couldn't understand my math problems. You put down your newspaper to help me. Thank you for helping me.

Child 2: I asked you to help me with my reading. You said, "I'm busy." I learned everything in your life is more important than I am.

Child 1: You promised to take me to the zoo if I brought up my grades. I did, and you did.

Child 2: You promised to take me to a movie if I left you alone all afternoon. I went away, but when I came back, you were gone. I learned not to trust.

Child 1: I asked for a hug; you gave me a hug and a kiss. Thank you for loving me.

Child 2: I needed a hug; you pushed me away. I learned I'm not lovable.

Child 1: When I made a mistake, you forgave me.

Child 2: When I made a mistake, you hit me. I learned to hide my mistakes—or hit first.

Child 1: I learned that I should do to others what they have done to me *(freeze).*

Child 2: I learned that I should do to others what they have done to me *(freeze).*

Adult: *(reads the following, another of the above passages, or any other appropriate scripture)* Jesus said, "Let the little children come to me, and do not hinder them, for the kingdom of heaven belongs to such as these."

MY GOD, MY CRITIC, AND ME

Contemporary Skit

SCRIPTURE: Psalm 34:18, Psalm 51:17, Proverbs 22:10, Matthew 11:18, 1 John 3:18-20.

THEME: When we condemn ourselves for our failures, God loves us enough to use those failures to bring us joy.

PRESENTERS: Three adults or youth.

SUGGESTED SETTING: The presenter representing **The Lord** might enter at first speech or be standing/sitting frozen or with back to the congregation until time to speak. **Critic** might stand or sit slightly behind **Me**, so **Critic** represents part of that person and not a separate being.

PRESENTATION

(Optional: the following can be read before or after the drama skit or can be printed in the bulletin as a thought for the day.)

Reader: We all have a little voice inside that tells us when to worry, when to fear, when to be ashamed. A friendly critic may help keep us out of trouble. A fearful critic stifles us. It's this little critic that keeps us from trying again when we don't succeed the first time. It's this voice that tells us not to take risks. It's this voice that keeps us from the very God who will free us from its scorn. Proverbs 22:10 tells us what to do about this kind of critic. "Drive out the mocker, and out goes strife; quarrels and insults are ended." Drive out the Mocker, welcome the Comforter, and live a new life.

Critic: Where are you going? I'm your Critic. You can't go without me.

Me: I'm taking my failures to the Lord. I'm going to kneel and lay them at his feet. Because I'm so sorry.

Critic: You can't do that! You should be ashamed to meet his gaze. Look away!

Me: I will not look at the Lord. I will bow my head in disgrace. Perhaps I will receive pity.

Critic: What you will get is rebuke.

Me: It is what I deserve, I know.

Critic: You have wasted far too much time trying to achieve what was clearly not within your grasp.

Me: I didn't know it wasn't within my grasp.

Critic: You should have known.

Me: Maybe I will be forgiven.

Critic: Do you forgive yourself?

Me: No.

Critic: I rest my case.

Me: I have to do something. I'm going.

Critic: Fool.

Me: I lay my failures at your feet, O Lord. I do not dare look at you, but I ask, forgive me.

Critic: I'm telling you—what you deserve is a stern lecture, not forgiveness. But wait, what is he doing? I don't understand this. He's gathering up your failures, all of them. The battered, misshapen, flawed efforts, and . . .

Me: He is laying them on his altar, so gently. He's treating them like precious gifts.

Critic: Why?

Me: O Lord, please! Hide them away! At your altar should lie the gifts of triumph, the precious and beautiful and the pure. Not failures like these.

The Lord: My child, these are not failures.

Critic: Yes they are. Look at them.

The Lord: I'm not talking to you.

Critic: Oh . . . sorry.

The Lord: Didn't you do your best to reach your goal?

Me: Yes.

The Lord: Then how can these be failures?

Critic: For one thing, the goals weren't accomplished. The people didn't get it. They didn't do what they were supposed to do.

Me: I failed.

The Lord: Maybe they failed.

Me: But the result of this project was supposed to be . . .

The Lord: You are not responsible for the results.

Critic: But . . .

The Lord: You are only responsible for the process.

Me: What have I accomplished then?

Critic: Yeah, what, I'd like to know.

The Lord: You've sown a seed. Whether anything grows is not up to you.

Critic: Good grief, there isn't much challenge in that, running around sowing seeds.

Me: I like it.

Critic: You still have to figure out which ones to sow and where to sow them and all that. You can't handle it alone, I'll bet.

Me: I'm not alone.

Critic: Well, yes, I'll help.

Me: I didn't mean you.

Critic: Oh.

Me: You hold me back. God leads me forward.

Critic: But I'm the most important part about you.

Me: Not any more.

*(The forgiven and God depart together, leaving the **Critic** to look on bewildered; he then runs after them or slinks off in the other direction.)*

A CONVERSATION WITH JESUS

Contemporary Scripture Skit

SCRIPTURE: John 4:10-26
THEME: Believe and do the will of God, a modern adaptation of the Woman at the Well.
PRESENTERS: Jesus and one to three readers.

PRESENTATION

Reader: *(sitting alone, head down, on stool)*

Jesus: *(calls either from out of sight with a microphone or in view. The name used here is Rachel, but the reader can be called any name, his or her own or one made up that suits better.)*

Jesus: Rachel.

Reader: *(remains with head down)*

Jesus: Rachel.

Reader: *(looks up but doesn't respond)*

Jesus: Rachel.

Reader: What! What can you want of me?

Jesus: Will you help me to rescue the homeless?

Reader: Why do you ask me to do this? I am not qualified.

Jesus: Will you help me to feed the hungry?

Reader: I am working day and night to feed my family. You know I haven't the time.

Jesus: Will you help me to comfort those who suffer terrible illness?

Reader: Why do you ask me, of all people, knowing how I fear contagious diseases?

Jesus: Will you help me to teach the violent better ways to live?

Reader: This is a hopeless task you ask of me.

Jesus: If you believed in the power of God, you would have given me all I asked; for you would be given the power to do all and more.

Reader: Are you so great as all that? If so, why do you need me? Why do you not rescue and feed and comfort and teach by yourself?

Jesus: Because I love you, and I want to give you my power. You believe in the power of the world, but it is temporary. Whoever believes in the power of the world will be left sad and lonely. Believe in me, accept the spirit of power and truth, and you will never be sad and lonely again.

Reader: You are a prophet. No one disputes that. But some worship here, some there. Some, this way, some, that. What is right?

Jesus: You worship me, but you do not know me. Not really. For if you knew me, you would know the place you worship and the method

	is neither right nor wrong. What is right is to worship in spirit and truth.
Reader:	Some day, I will know the truth.
Jesus:	The day has come. The time is now. I am the Messiah, your savior. I will teach you if you will hear.
Reader:	But, Lord, I am a sinner.
Jesus:	You are a sinner.
Reader:	I am not worthy.
Jesus:	You are so worthy that I would give my life for you.

EPIPHANY

Contemporary Skit

SCRIPTURE: Matthew 2:1-12
THEME: What is epiphany?
PRESENTERS: Two adults, one child and one adult, or two children or youth
Character 1 is childlike and enthusiastic, rather pumped up with knowledge of the story and teacher role.
Character 2 is determined to stick to the facts, to the proof of the matter.
Presenters for Optional Reading: as many as desired.
ADDITION SUGGESTIONS FOR THE SERVICE: Altar or communion table decoration consists of something gold and containers appropriate for frankincense and myrrh. These may already be in place or may be

brought in by dancers during the singing of "We Three Kings."

DIRECTOR'S NOTE: *Two presenters read this skit dramatically. The skit can be followed with a sermon or message about personal epiphanies, when people experience a revelation or feel the presence of God or recognize the divine in their own lives. The message can be followed by the reading "Go Tell It," which follows the skit.*

PRESENTATION

1:   We're going to tell you the story of the Magi.

2:   That would be epiphany.

1:   What's *epiphany?*

2:   An illuminating discovery. A revealing moment or scene, an appearance or manifestation of a divine being.

1:   The story of the Magi.

2:   The story of the Magi.

1:   Okay. The Magi were kings and they . . .

2:   No, they weren't.

1:   Yes, they were, and they came out of their palaces one day, and they saw a bright star that pointed to Bethle . . .

2:   No, they didn't . . .

1:   Didn't what?

2:   Didn't live in palaces or see a bright star pointing to Bethlehem. They had to go to King Herod to find out that Jesus was in Bethlehem. And nobody said anything about palaces.

1:   Kings live in palaces.

2: They weren't kings. They were just wise men. Legend has it they were . . .

1: Never mind about legends. Now! King Herod was really mad when he heard about a king being born because he was suspicious and wicked, and so the kings were really scared of him, but . . .

2: They weren't scared of him. They didn't know that he was wicked.

1: Who's telling this story *(2 may try to answer or shrug)*. So Herod called his priests and scribes to find out if what the kings said was true—that there was a new king born. They told him Jesus had been born in Bethlehem.

2: No they didn't.

1: Yes, they did.

2: They told him the prophets said a Christ would be born in Bethlehem. They didn't know about Jesus. They were just talking in general from what the scriptures said.

1: So Herod sent the kings to Bethlehem to search for the baby.

2: Which wouldn't be easy. Bethlehem was about as big as Chicago.

1: It doesn't say anything about Chicago in the Bible.

2: Finding the baby wouldn't be easy, that's all I'm saying.

1: And then they were to come back and tell Herod, so that he could worship him.

2: Not worship him, kill him. That's what Herod really wanted to do.

1: So the kings went to Bethlehem and followed the star right to the manger...

2: House.

1: House? Jesus wasn't born in a house.

2: No, but by now he is resting in a house with his mom. You don't think he stayed in a cave forever, do you?

1: The kings bowed down and worshiped him.

2: They did.

1: And they gave him presents. Gold, frankincense...

2: Incense...

1: and myrrh.

2: Used for embalming the dead.

1: The kings wouldn't give a baby embalming fluid.

2: It was very valuable in those days.

1: And then they went away and they all dreamed...

2: *(Interrupts)* Maybe just one dreamed that...

1: *(Continues as if no interruption)* that they should not go back to Herod.

1: And so they returned to their country by another route.

2: They did.

GO TELL IT

Epiphany Skit

(This skit may follow the Epiphany dialogue at the end of the service or may stand alone.)

SCRIPTURE: Matthew 2:1-12

Reader 1: Wise men followed a star.

Reader 2: Or maybe it was a nudge or gossip they responded to.

Reader 3: They believed and left gifts of respect and received nothing in return.

Reader 1: Only later would we all learn that the gifts Jesus wants from us are not valuables such as gold and jewelry, but to tend to the needs of others.

Reader 2: But we do receive something in return. We receive the gift of faith.

Reader 3: And it does glitter. It is bright.

Reader 1: It is the most valuable thing we own.

Reader 2: Others will see and desire what we have, and they won't know how to get it unless we tell them.

Reader 3: Tell them.

PALM SUNDAY

Drama and Movement for Children and Adults

SCRIPTURE: John 12:13 and verses from Matthew 23.
THEME: Jesus illustrates the paradox of a feared and hated man who was at the same time loved, admired, and welcomed.
PRESENTERS: Six adults for brief memorized parts, three children for movement and memorized speaking parts. Optional: 1 child or youth dancer
PROPS: One or two palms for each child
COSTUMES: If lines are memorized, adults could wear biblical garments or dress all in black or gray. By contrast, children should wear very colorful clothes.
DIRECTOR'S NOTE: *This short drama with movement works best if it introduces the Palm Sunday service when the children traditionally bring in the palms.*

PRESENTATION

*(The **Pharisees, Sadducees,** and **Zealots** may enter and take places, grouped a little way from each other; or they may be in place at the start of the service. When a couple is not speaking, the two cross their arms over their chests and remain frozen, looking stern.)*

Pharisee 1:   Vipers! This Jesus calls us vipers.

Pharisee 2:   We are the Pharisees. We follow every law, every tradition handed down from Moses. We keep ourselves pure and holy.

Pharisee 1:   He calls us hypocrites. Us!

Pharisee 2:   Who does he think he is. He's not even educated. Not like us *(freeze).*

Sadducee 1:   He criticizes us too. The Sadducees. He ignores our power and derides our position.

Sadducee 2: We rule here. We intercede with Rome. We arbitrate and compromise.

Sadducee 1: He mocks us because we are wealthy.

Sadducee 2: He is nothing but a troublemaker.

Sadducee 1: A revolutionary *(freeze)*.

Zealot 1: He is not a revolutionary.

Zealot 2: He is a fool.

Zealot 1: He says, "Turn the other cheek if your enemy strikes you."

Zealot 2: He says, "Give to Caesar what's Caesar's."

Zealot 1: He's a fool. Don't worry about him. A fool has few followers.

Sadducee 1: He will be forgotten.

Pharisee 1: This Jesus is a nobody.

All: Nobody!

(Optional Dancers: One or more children dance into the sanctuary with palms to any joyful music appropriate for Palm Sunday. Choreography should be simple but joyous with a combination of skips, twirls, and leaps, followed by a reverent bowing as if to a king, then a repeat of the skips, twirls, and leaps. The child or children may dance all the way to the front of the sanctuary and take positions where they remain throughout the rest of the children's dance, or they may dance back out of the sanctuary.)

Child 1: *(Enters and takes a place from where he or she can be seen and heard. If it is necessary for the child to cover some distance to get to the place of speaking, maybe before a microphone, the child should skip or run with excitement.* **Child 1** *does an*

excited twirl, stops to call loudly.) Hosanna!
Hosanna in the highest! *(This line may be
repeated as **Child** moves to the front.)*

*(Twirls with palm in hand, skips and lays palm down at the
altar or other designated place. Kneels, facing
congregation.)*

Child 2: *(Enters carrying palm forward on outstretched arms
with much dignity)* Blessed is he who comes
in the name of the Lord.
(Takes palm to designated place, then kneels.)

Child 3: Blessed is the King of Israel. Blessed is the
King of Israel.

*(**Child 3** places palm and goes to **Child 1** and
Child 2, who rise and follow **Child 3**. All hold
hands in a chain. **Child 3,** leading the other
two, walks to the group of adults who have stood
frozen all this time and circles them. When coming back to the front of the group, the children
stop and recite the following, facing the congregation. The adults do not move until indicated.)*

Child 1: Jesus said you should come to God as little
children.

*(The **Pharisees** turn sharply and walk out.)*

Child 2: Jesus said that it is easier for a camel to get
through the eye of a needle than for a rich
man to see God.

*(The **Sadducees** turn and walk out.)*

Child 3: Jesus said to love other people—ALL other
people—and you will have peace.

*(The **Zealots** turn and walk out.)*

Child 1: *(Raising both arms above head)* Hosanna. Hosanna
in the highest.

Child 2: *(Raising both arms above head)* Blessed is he who comes in the name of the Lord.

Child 3: *(Raising both arms above head)* Blessed is the king of Israel.

All 3 Children: Hosanna! Hosanna! *(All **Children** enter carrying palms. These children should be led by an older child or teenager who knows exactly what to do and where to go. They may circle the altar or walk in from any door of the sanctuary and proceed directly to seats with palms in hands. Most anything will work if the children are led by one or more confident, knowledgeable older children.)*

Chapter Three

SACRED DANCE

Let the people of Zion be glad in their King. Let them praise his name with dancing.

—Psalm 149:2*b*-3*a*

A celebration of life and God, a spiritual act—sacred dance is the Holy Spirit within manifested in observable motion. It is spirit in motion. Every gesture, expression, and action says something about our relationship with God. Sacred dance is not, however, movement for movement's sake, no matter how beautiful that may be, nor is it movement to impress an audience with the dancer's skills, regardless of how awesome that might be.

Sacred dance interprets a scripture, illustrates a theme, communicates a feeling, brings the Holy Spirit into motion. Some of our most intense emotions are best, and certainly more easily, expressed through movement. Think about what you do with your body when you are angry, afraid, joyful, thankful, and sorrowful. What do you do with your arms? your hands? your head and torso?

You can watch a child and, without hearing a word, know what he or she is feeling. Life is lived through motion. To limit movement within worship as we have done for centuries is to neglect a natural method of worshiping God and sharing the gospel with each other. Some people are spiritually touched by sacred dance both as participants and observers; while for others, restricting movement in worship actually prevents them from growing to full capacity spiritually.

We might surmise from the negative attitudes many people have concerning dance in worship that scripture forbids movement and fervent expression of feeling through the body, but this is not the case. The Bible makes specific references to dance in Psalm 30:11, Psalm 150, and Exodus 15:20. Jesus also refers to dancing in Matthew 11:17 and Luke 15:25.

THE BENEFITS OF DANCE IN WORSHIP

For many, the spirit speaks through movement, not words. Even those who prefer other modes of sacred expression are uplifted by an exuberant, colorful, joyous dance to an Easter anthem. Dance may reach all of us in some way because the connections we make in movement are more pure, without the analytical thought processes that come into play when we speak.

THE CALL TO THE LEAST QUALIFIED

With dance even more than with drama, we tend to think years of training and talent are essential to a presentation before a public gathering, and this may be true—for professional dance. Sacred dance, however, is a method of worship that focuses on the internal and the spiritual, making technique and form less important. This means that even though a person has little dance training, he or she may direct a sacred dance program.

Perhaps someone in your church has dance training and wants to dance liturgically and has the time and likes to teach. If not, and you are coordinated and rhythmic, you may either have to direct a newly formed sacred dance troupe yourself or find someone else to do so. At times, we all feel like Moses, and want to yell, "Choose someone else!" But if God is calling you to speak to those people whose spirits hear best through sacred movement, shouldn't you accept the call in faith and know that you will not be without his guidance anymore than Moses was?

INTRODUCING SACRED MOVEMENT INTO WORSHIP

Hire a Choreographer

How do you start? You begin a dance program with a dance, of course. However, until you can choreograph your own dance, you may want to hire someone else to do it for you. There are several ways to find a choreographer of sacred movement. First, contact churches in your area that include sacred dance in worship and ask for the name and phone number of the choreographer or director. Second, attend sacred dance workshops and consult the leader. Third, check the yellow pages for dance studios that offer classes in liturgical or sacred dance. Finally, call professional dance companies that include modern dance in their repertoire.

Once contacted, the choreographer will need to know if music has already been selected for the movement and the date the dancers will be presenting the dance in worship. He or she will want to know if you expect a dance troupe to be brought into the church to present the dance or if you expect him or her to teach a dance to a group from your church. Compensation should correspond to the experience and training of the choreographer as well as to the length and complexity of the dance to be designed.

Beginning a dance program with an outside group of dancers allows the congregation to see the beauty and purity of feeling that defines sacred movement, without the worry of a long-term commitment to the idea. On the other hand, when the church's own members are dancing, there is ownership in the presentation. Most observers will be agreeable and supportive just because those dancing are a part of the church family. One choreographer's dance group consists of her church members combined with dancers from other churches and sometimes dancers from the church that hired her. For both the church and the new dancers, this is an ideal way to create interest in sacred dance.

As for finding dancers, see chapter 1, page 20, "Seeking Presenters." Suffice it to say that once people who love movement have participated in sacred dance, they will want to repeat the experience. Continually nurtured, the dancers taking those first tentative steps will bloom into a dance troupe that will enhance worship on a regular basis.

Where and How to Learn Choreography

Attending sacred dance workshops and classes will help enormously and is probably the best way to learn how to choreograph dances. In most instances, you will gather ideas for interpretive movement, practice beginning choreography, and often learn a dance or two that you can teach to others.

Another way to learn is to observe a professional or semi-professional dance company that does interpretive movement. While you may not acquire specific steps, you will almost certainly come away inspired with ideas for costuming, working with props, and music.

Studying the numerous books on sacred dance is another excellent way to learn since they offer music suggestions and provide specific movements and gestures as well as choreography for entire dances. Two books that are especially helpful are Carla De Sola's *The Spirit Moves* and *Look Up and Live* by Margaret Taylor (see appendix B).

Any book that illustrates basic ballet positions and movements can be helpful, since looking at the drawings and trying to mimic them will reawaken your own creativity in regard to movement.

Dancing for another choreographer is one of the best ways to develop your own skills. When you hire a choreographer to direct a dance at your church, be the first person to sign up. If the opportunity presents itself, dance for other choreographers at other churches. By rehearsing a certain movement or gesture over and over for a dance, you are likely to find that movement incorporated in your own repertoire. With the choreographer's permission, you can recreate the entire dance at your own church with your dancers. Finally, the simple experience of dancing before a congregation builds confidence. If you can do it at someone else's church, you can certainly do it at your own.

CREATING MOVEMENT

Create Your Own Movement

The time has come to create your own movement, and you're probably saying, "I'm not ready for this." Yes, you are, but here are a few tips: Learn what your body can and cannot do. Accept your limitations, but do not assume that because you can't pirouette or touch your toes that you cannot express yourself spiritually through movement. If you don't exercise, begin now. Reacquaint your body with the joy of movement. Exercise to music that touches your soul. According to Terese Chatelaine, choreographer and director of Jubilate Liturgical Dance, exercise is sacred movement if it is born of the spirit. So exercise your body and your spirit at the same time.

Interpret a Psalm

As with the instructions on drama, begin simply. At first, interpret a short psalm or several verses of a longer one. Select material that contains strong emotion, clear visual images, and dynamic verbs. If you can feel or see it, you can move to it. Select the verses that best exemplify the theme of the worship service. During movement, the psalm may be read by someone not dancing or recited by the dancers as they move. You may want to provide a musical background with meditation music, a flute, cello, violin, or drum.

Tell a Scripture Story

While a narrator reads or recites, dance the scripture. Start by miming the actions and feelings of the text, then elaborate on the movements, making them more fluid.

Combine Hymns and Movement

As with psalms, select a hymn with clear visual images and a rhythmic, danceable beat. The "Hymn of Promise" and "There's a Song in the Air" work well for beginning movement with images that include flowers and butterflies bursting from cocoons; songs soaring in the air, stars raining down, a mother's prayer, and a manger cradling a king. Refer to signing and dance books for help duplicating the gestures and movements, then elaborate on or alter them to suit your style and your dance. (See appendix B, pages 194-97 for resources and workshop leaders.)

Dance a Prayer

Dancing a prayer is not difficult since sacred movement is prayer. In addition, this is a good way to try abstract movement, which is more difficult than choreographing to specific words or phrases. In abstract movement, you are dancing a feeling or emotion, which is often the essence of prayer. Let other dancers help in movement to prayer by having them express with their bodies such feelings as love, joy, sorrow, anguish, desire, praise, and fear in as many ways as they can think of. The most expressive of these movements can be written or drawn, practiced, and presented in worship.

— SUGGESTED MOVEMENTS —

Some gestures and movements are born of natural bodily responses to certain feelings and visual images:

- A hand to the heart illustrates love;
- Arms raised praise God;
- Palms cupped upward receive;
- Hands before the eyes signify blindness or being in the dark;
- Twirling in a circle signifies joy;
- Slow walking, head bowed, shows sorrow.

Allowing your natural creativity to come into play and elaborating on these and other basic movements can help in choreographing a dance.

Experiment with the following:

- The hand at the heart may be open or closed in a fist to illustrate anguish;
- It may rise and fall several times, beating the breast in anguish;
- It may move from an open palm against the chest outward and up, palm open to the heavens, giving God your love.

The body speaks through posture as well as movement:

- A body curled in on itself feels sorrow;
- Collapsing all the way to the floor illustrates that a burden is too heavy to carry;
- Backing away demonstrates fear; moving forward with eager, certain steps conveys confidence and joy;
- Arms extended forward and crossed at the wrists with palms facing forward and head turned sideways wards off a threat;
- Crossing the wrists and pulling the arms in with palms cupped slightly; head down gives a vulnerable, humble look.

What makes movement dance is technique. When a dancer walks, she or he doesn't just clump the feet down, arms dangling, but rather positions the head, arms, shoulders, and facial expression in such a way as to convey a certain feeling. Joyful movements are more rapid, open, and elevated than sorrowful movements that tend to be slow, closed in on the self, and dropped. This is easy to visualize if you consider how a person acts when happy as opposed to when depressed.

When creating a movement, a choreographer may use mirrors to decide what is effective and appealing. An audiotaped version of the music that can be stopped and started often is necessary as is space in which to move. Early in the process, you can work at home, but later preparation should be done in the sanctuary if possible.

Unless a dance is a solo piece, you will need to teach others what you have choreographed. Careful note taking as you create each step is essential. Even if you memorize the complete dance, it can be difficult to remember whether you are starting left or right or using the left or right hand and foot in a particular spot without written notes.

Don't be afraid to change a movement if you don't like what you see or if the group finds it awkward or too difficult. Although the dancers may find these changes annoying, the dance is bound to look better.

Interpret with a Group Creation

A group of people can interpret a psalm in a unique, personal, and effective manner. This method of interpretation is much easier for the director and can provide inspiration, fellowship, and a sense of creative pride for the group. Select a portion of scripture, assign a verse or two to each individual in the group or, with a large group, form several clusters and assign a verse or two to each cluster. Give everyone five or ten minutes to create movements to the assigned scripture before coming together to share their creations.

As one person reads, each cluster interprets the verses.

Have the group stand in a semicircle and repeat the series of movements with each cluster freezing in place after their verses are completed. By the end of the reading, you will have an impressive tableau of worship gestures.

Improvise

Improvisation is moving to an inner voice, sound, feeling, or rhythm. As children, most of us did this naturally; but as adults, the messages outside ourselves tend to drown out these internal sensors. The structure that we have been compelled to live within has inhibited our natural movements. For some of us, creativity has shriveled to the point of disappearing altogether, and it is hard to recapture.

My mother tells the story that when I was very small, I danced to the rhythmic sound of the washing machine. When I first started teaching high school, I remember standing next to an old copier positively itching to swing shoulders and hips to the pulsating beat of paper being disgorged. I didn't. What would the office secretary, other teachers, or worse, the principal think?

That what-will-people-think syndrome is what makes improvisation difficult for some of us. To improvise a sacred dance is to get back in touch with your inner rhythms, ignoring the voices that come from without.

Do the following experiment before attempting to choreograph a dance based on your improvisations or before dancing in a group.

In a room where you will be uninterrupted, on your knees or standing, listen to music that moves you internally.

At first, simply listen and allow the music to speak to you.

Begin to move, letting the music establish your mood and the rapidity with which you move. Sway your

---

body, reach up to God with one hand, then the other, then both. Raise and lower your arms gracefully, thinking of bird wings. Press your palms down toward the ground or out from your heart, pushing away what burdens you; lift your palms from the heart to the skies, giving God your love. Turn in circles feeling the joy of life. Move in any way the music or your emotion leads you. Exercise every appendage and every muscle in your body, including neck, wrists, and ankles. Do it all to the music, eyes closed or nearly so. Finish by sitting or kneeling quietly. Note the way you feel, the way your body feels.

Dance instructor and choreographer Melli Hoppe offers a workshop in which participants create their own individual spiritual paths, first walking them, then adding movement that suggests where they are at any given point on the path. Participants are also asked to create a personal sacred gesture, then make the gesture abstract by expanding on it, and then elaborate still further on the abstraction. A choreographed dance comes from combining all of the above movements into a set combination.

Attending workshops facilitated by dancers who specialize in improvisational movement is probably the best way to learn to choreograph by improvising to music. There are so many approaches to sacred dance and so many wonderful teachers that you will not only learn but come away inspired and full of courage to try something new. Ballet, interpretive, and modern dance training are helpful for personal body conditioning and flexibility, and they are also important to your church ministry since they provide a larger repertoire of movements from which to draw when choreographing.

Work with Props

In sacred dance, a more appropriate word for props might be *symbols* since most items featured within a dance are used to symbolize an emotion, object, or event. A hoop with ribbons tied to it symbolizes joy; flowers may represent a season or innocence; swords can be manipulated in a dance to convey the soldiers' role on Good Friday.

Good Friday provides one of the best opportunities for movement with symbols since the bag of coins, bowl and pitcher, whip, crown of thorns, nails, sponge or chalice, dice, and INRI sign tell the story of the crucifixion without vocal accompaniment. The way presenters move when bringing in and placing the symbols reveals how they feel about them. A grieving Mary will relate to the crown of thorns much differently than a soldier.

The use of fabric of all kinds can benefit a movement. A lengthy strip of cloth might represent a shroud at Easter, folded into a bundle it appears to be a baby at Christmas. Flowing chiffon in blues, greens, and grays may illustrate water.

One of the most effective ways to use fabric on Good Friday is to cover all of the Easter flowers and/or the cross and then remove the cloth with joyful exuberance at the beginning of an Easter dance or processional. If the lights have been dimmed and then are brought up at the same time that the flowers are revealed, the effect will be that the sun illuminated the flowers at dawn much like that first Easter.

Mary Bell, a choreographer who often uses fabric as symbols, suggests that dancers experiment with long pieces of cloth. Holding the ends, the dancers can move forward and back with the cloth, lifting and lowering it; roll inward toward each other; and then wrap each other in the cloth. In one of her dances, four dancers hold a long, narrow gold cloth, which represents good, while four others carry a dark piece of fabric, which represents evil. The two sets of cloth-carrying dancers rush toward each other in rhythmic intervals illustrating the tug-of-war that goes on between good and evil.

She has choreographed a dance that features camouflage netting found in an army surplus store, which becomes a fishermen's net, and another one where a long piece of gauze, representing a shroud, is stretched over the heads of the congregation sitting in their pews. As part of movement, she has dancers set communion tables with heavy linenlike material or manipulate shimmering fabric, which represents rivers, clouds, and wind.

Dancers may lead processionals down the center aisle of the sanctuary carrying banners or otherwise introduce a worship service. For example, on Easter a dancer may enter the sanctuary, the first thing in the service, swathed in black cloth and then remove the cloth to reveal white, bright colors, or pastels, which represent the dawn of new life in the Resurrection.

Except for chiffon, most materials can and should be inexpensive. By planning ahead, finer fabrics can be purchased when they are on sale.

CHILDREN'S DANCES

Working with a group of children will generally require greater effort than working with a group of adults. It is unlikely that you will be able to work consistently with children under five years of age, since their attention spans are extremely short; they often are not yet coordinated sufficiently to do even simple movements, and they may be unwilling to do in worship what they learned in rehearsal.

One way to include younger children in dances more often is to have an older child lead a chain of children who are holding hands. This allows little ones to be brought into the sanctuary at the pace you desire and to be deposited where you want them. If you have the right ratio, a young child or two can stand slightly behind an older one and model his or her movements.

Most children's music is already danceable, while some practically choreographs itself. For example, Mary Rice-Hopkins' "Easter Rise Up" is a delightful song for children to dance to that already includes instructions for them to follow: "Stand up, turn around, touch the ground." The words also instruct the children to dance and sing and perform other motions.

Another simple idea is to tie any number of colorful ribbons onto the wrists of the little dancers and have them raise and lower their arms, turn with arms above their heads, and circle around while holding hands. Sign language also works well with young children. They can usually manage hand and arm signs more easily than fancy footwork. It's the arm and hand movements and those wonderful faces that the congregation longs to see.

It is very important that children are praised often, especially during rehearsals, and that they are not criticized harshly for mistakes. On the other hand, there is nothing wrong with expecting each child to give his or her best. Rehearsal time that occurs in an atmosphere that is free of distractions, including multiple repetitions, gentle correction, and lots of genuine praise while deleting what is too difficult will encourage children to do their best.

SACRED MOVEMENT FOR THE PHYSICALLY OR GRACEFULLY CHALLENGED

Unless your dancers are all young and agile, each will be dealing with some form of physical hindrance. It may be as simple as a lack of flexibility that makes bending gracefully difficult or it may be as challenging as paralysis in the lower extremities. A person in her seventies might be unable to get down on her knees. A stout man might not be able to pirouette or rise onto his toes. Some people are gracefully challenged. Their body builds and natural awkwardness make attaining grace and poise a constant, difficult battle. Regardless of their physical impediments, most people can worship God with their bodies and any who wish to do sacred movement should be welcomed to participate.

The physically challenged cannot participate in every sacred dance, but they can be a part of those movements that involve the areas of the body where they have mobility. If it is clear from the start that movement in worship is a spiritual activity and not a performance, people who have always wanted to dance but thought they couldn't will participate and be touched in unsuspected ways. A seventy-one-year-old dancer once said, "I thought my dancing days were over. What a joy to use my body again to interpret the Lord's Prayer."

FINDING DANCERS

When you start your program, avoid using the word *dance* since many people have preconceived ideas about dancing. A better description is *sacred movement*. Invite anyone interested in the interpretation of scripture and hymns through movement to meet at a certain time when you will explain the program in more detail. Assure people that there are no age, gender, or experience restrictions and no obligation for attending an informational meeting about the program.

At the meeting, define sacred movement and clarify how this form of worship benefits both the presenter and the congregation. If possible, demonstrate a short sacred movement piece or show a video. (Bear in mind that a video of professional dancers might discourage people rather than inspire them to try.) Also explain what you would like to do, for example, present an interpretation of one psalm on a given Sunday or form an ongoing sacred movement group.

Present your first movement and include all of the participants, whether it's one or ten. If no one agrees to participate, then dance alone. Almost certainly, at least one other person will join you after seeing the initial presentation.

Be patient. Many people are slow starters, needing to see a number of movement presentations in worship before they have the nerve to try it themselves. This is one reason to include sacred movement in worship fairly regularly. Don't hesitate to ask people personally, especially men, teenagers, seniors, and the physically challenged who you think might be both able and interested in movement of this kind. Their responses will depend largely on how complicated the dances appear that you've been doing in worship.

REHEARSALS

For in-depth information on the basic format of preparation meetings, refer to chapter 1 (pages 21-22) and the exercises listed in appendix A. Meetings should last no less than one and one-half hours, allowing for prayer, warm-up exercises, and rehearsal of the piece. Allow about an hour of rehearsal time per one minute of music or one verse of a hymn. Inexperienced dancers learn best by watching and imitating. Avoid teaching too much at once. Instead, repeat a brief combination of movements before going on to the next, using this pattern until the whole dance is learned. Use the last rehearsal as an opportunity to review and polish the entire dance and to focus on facial expressions that may have previously consisted of concentrated frowns. It is also a good idea to rehearse in costume before the service in order to become accustomed to kneeling and rising without tripping in long skirts. In addition, dress rehearsals illustrate where swishing skirts come close to upsetting flowers, plants, statues, or candles or when the ribbons of swinging hoops are likely to touch the faces of those sitting in the front pews. Finally, ill-fitting costumes can be altered if the problem is discovered several days in advance of Sunday worship.

Although a professional presentation is not the goal, it is important for everyone involved to do their best, to be comfortable with what they are doing, and to enjoy the experience if the congregation is to receive the greatest benefit.

After the presentation, thank the presenters for sharing their faith through movement. Remember when errors occur to sympathize, not minimize, to share your own past mistakes, and to remind the presenters that they are called not to be perfect but to be spiritual. Repeat what, hopefully, you have told them in rehearsal, that the congregation often doesn't know what's right or wrong in the movement.

ADAPTING MOVEMENT

Adapt the movements in the dances at the end of this chapter to your sanctuary environment, the capabilities of your dancers, and your own creative desires. Note dancers who have difficulty performing a particular movement and those who cannot do it at all. However, don't be too hasty to change things. Some people will need a little practice, while others will need quite a bit more. Although the dances should not be so difficult that people can't enjoy them, most adults reap a tremendous sense of accomplishment when they master a difficult movement.

Obviously the same suggestion works for the director as for the dancers. If you don't understand a suggestion for a movement, don't care for it, or can't do it, make suitable changes.

MUSIC

Music may be provided by a choir, soloists, a piano, an organ, or any other instrument, including drums. Tapes and CDs also can be used to provide music. Live music is often preferable but there are two drawbacks: You will need a tape of the hymn or song before you start rehearsing in order to choreograph; and once the dancers learn the dance to that tape, the live music may be faster or slower which results in on-the-spot adapting of the rhythm. A major disadvantage to using tapes and CDs is the dependence on a mechanical unit that may malfunction at a critical time. Be sure to check equipment immediately before a worship service.

If you do not read music and/or possess a limited repertoire of music, enlist the assistance of a choir director, organist, or others who are knowledgeable about various types of music. There is probably someone within your congregation who has a fine collection of classical music or spirituals or jazz who could help you find the right background music for a movement. Members of your congregation who play a musical instrument might provide the accompaniment you need or might at least suggest a suitable piece.

In addition to consulting music lovers in your congregation, other excellent ways to find suitable music for dancing include borrowing tapes from the public library, browsing religious bookstores, and perusing your hymnal.

CONGREGATIONAL INVOLVEMENT

If you wish for the congregation to take part in a movement piece, select a short song or prayer they already know so that they can concentrate on the movement without having to look at their hymnals. Teach them the signs or gestures, and tell them to follow the dancers. Assure them they need not participate if they are uncomfortable. Repeat the same song or prayer every Sunday for several weeks to familiarize everyone with the signs. After a while you will notice that most of the congregation will sign as automatically as they sing.

STAGING

When you are staging a dance, it is important to remember that what is pleasing to look at is not totally dependent on the combination of steps and gestures of the dancers. If the chancel area has more than one level, interesting patterns may be created by having a dancer or dancers perform the same movements on each level. Dancers may move in a circle, a straight line, a double line, a V formation, staggered, or in no apparent formation at all. They may dance up and down the aisles, around an altar, or on a balcony.

Dancers may also move in unison, progressively, randomly, some in slow motion, others fast, shadowing a partner, or mirroring one. Having various dancers freeze in positions representing different aspects of worship and holding those positions for a short period may have an indelible effect on the congregation. In other words, movement doesn't need to be complicated to be effective.

COSTUMING

Dancers have a variety of options when it comes to costumes. They can wear lightweight warm-up pants of like colors and white T-shirts, or mixed colors of T-shirts and pants. Long-sleeved white blouses and shirts with black pants or skirts work well for many types of movement.

Costumes should be made of washable, relatively wrinkle-proof, opaque, lightweight, flowing material. Circle skirts in basic colors such as white or purple are extremely functional.

The following is an idea adopted from liturgical dancer and choreographer, Mary Bell: Leave an opening in the waistband of a skirt with the elastic protruding through and safety pinned; this makes the skirt wearable by women of several different sizes. Tops can be made simply by cutting a hole in the center of one and one-half to two yards of a pretty fabric and hemming all edges. Snaps can be sewn in the sides to make arm holes or the sides can be safety pinned.

HINTS FOR USING THE DANCE SCRIPTS

1. When speakers other than the dancers are involved in the movement, their lines are in bold or highlighted, unless it is a narration prior to the dance.
2. All speaking parts may be read or memorized, though short lines are best memorized and long narrations are best read.
3. Suggested movements follow each speaking line.
4. Age, gender, and costuming suggestions are not mentioned in the dances unless specific directions are necessary. Throughout the dances, dancers are referred to by role or by the appropriate pronoun for that role.
5. The most important factor in the following movements is that the suggested motions are flexible and are easily changed. Sacred dance is most meaningful when it springs from the individual's personal relationship with God. Although a dancer or director may need to start with choreography that is created by others in order to learn and to gain confidence, the ultimate goal should be to create movement that is one's own spirit in motion.

MOVEMENTS

Bold or darkened text indicates spoken lines interspersed with movement.

Suggestions for learning the following choreography.

1. Read through the entire dance, visualizing each movement as well as the overall dance.
2. Reread or have someone else read the directions for each movement or each short combination of movements, and practice before going on to the next.
3. Learn only the segment you plan to teach next,

remembering to teach only a minute or less of the dance at one rehearsal.

4. Thoroughly familiarize yourself with or memorize the words or the "story line" of the portion of the dance you will be teaching next.

KEY TO THE DIAGRAMS AND SOME BASIC POSITIONS

- If not indicated, the position of the head as well as of the feet and the direction the dancer looks are left to the discretion of the dancer and director.
- *Upstage* designates the back of a presentation area and *downstage*, the front.
- A reminder that the following movements are suggestions only. Dancers and directors are encouraged to adapt and create anew.

KEY TO SKETCHES

BASIC FORMATIONS

A Formation

Loose A Formation

V Formation

Loose V Formation

HEAD POSITIONS

Position of the point (nose) within and jutting from the circle indicates the direction dancer is looking, not necessarily facing, as the body may be facing sideways and the head facing the audience.

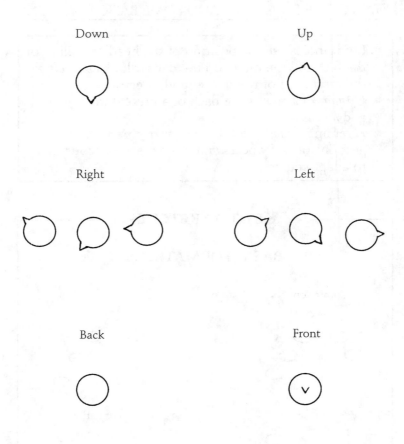

HAND POSITIONS

Palms forward

Palms back

Palms up

Palms in
(face each other)

Palms out
(Away from each other)

Palms flattened

Palms cupped

Prayer hands

Receiving hands

SPIRIT OF THE LIVING GOD

Congregational Movement to Hymn

PARTICIPANTS: One or more
MUSIC: "Spirit of the Living God"
DIRECTOR'S NOTE: *This song can be sung during worship before meditation and prayer for several weeks or months. Each time have the dancers demonstrate the movement to the congregation, one dancer standing before each section of pews.*

PRESENTATION

Spirit of the Living God, fall afresh on me.
Raise one arm very slowly. Bring hand down, wiggling fingers above head as if spirit is falling on head like rain. Lower hand in front of face continuing rain motion bringing to rest, palm in, on heart [Position 1, page 117].

Spirit of the living God, fall afresh on me.
Repeat above motions.
Melt me
Bring tips of fingers and thumbs together in a loose prayer hands position, at chest level and separate hands, downward and to sides, palms down, as if flattening and smoothing out.
Mold me
Bring hands toward each other as if holding a ball of clay and make molding motions.
Fill me
Bring finger tips together, palms flat and up, drawing hands close to chest and lifting from waist to heart level as if body is slowly filling with spirit [Position 2, page 117].

Use me
From heart level, move hands forward palms up.
Spirit of the living God, fall afresh on me.
Repeat above motions.

SERVICE OF THE LIGHT
EVENING MEDITATION SERVICE

Movement and Drama with Candles

MUSIC AND SCRIPTURE: Eleven scripture verses having to do with light: 1 John 1:5, Isaiah 60:20, Psalm 27:1, Psalm 119:105, John 1:4, John 8:12, 1 John 1:7, John 12:36, Ephesians 5:8, Matthew 5:16. Either no music or instrumental.

PARTICIPANTS: Narrator and one to four dancers, four to eleven candle carriers who also speak memorized lines. One narrator for the opening readings on darkness.

PROPS: One candle per scripture reader

LIGHTS: Lights are dim at the beginning or, if possible, begin with fairly bright lights and dim them bit by bit as each of the four movements representing darkness are presented. Darken the room completely just before the first candle carrier enters with a candle, and bring the lights back up only after the movement is completed.

DIRECTOR'S NOTE: *One dancer may present all the movements for the darkness recitation. Let dancer(s) experiment with movements illustrating fear, pain, and so forth. Candle carriers should be given the scripture they are to memorize before the first rehearsal, one verse of scripture per candle carrier. Willing candle carriers may learn more than one verse if there aren't enough people, or some of the verses may be deleted. Scripture reference may be mentioned or not as suits the director. This movement has been done successfully at the beginning of a Christmas Eve service.*

PRESENTATION

Narrator: In darkness uncertainty grows to fear, fear to terror.
Dancer moves in fear and freezes.

Narrator: In darkness pain takes on a new, more agonizing dimension.
Dancer moves in pain.

Narrator: In darkness we are not just lonely, but desolate and forsaken.
Dancer moves in loneliness.

Narrator: In darkness there is no direction; we are lost.
Dancer moves as if lost.

Narrator: We are all sometimes in darkness.
(Turn off all lights.)

Narrator: Why do you walk in darkness? You who are children of the light. Listen and believe.
Candle carriers enter completely darkened sanctuary one by one, carrying candles. They speak their lines after entering. They walk to designated positions in the sanctuary and remain.

Director may want to have candle carriers positioned so that they form a cross or just have them scattered around the sanctuary, front, sides, and back; or kneeling, standing, sitting on steps, and so forth to form a pleasing picture of light. Darkness dancers break positions and follow or join candle carriers as indicated by the director or as suggested here. The dancer may place a hand on the candle being carried by the carrier or on that person's arm, waist, or shoulder.

(Enter candle carriers.)

1: God is light; in him there is no darkness at all, 1 John 1:5. *(Pick up darkness dancer 1.)*

2: The Lord will be your everlasting light, Isaiah 60:20. *(Pick up darkness dancer 2.)*

3: The Lord is my light and my salvation, Psalm 27:1. *(Pick up darkness dancer 3.)*

4: Your word is a lamp to my feet and a light for my path, Psalm 119:105. *(Pick up darkness dancer 4.)*

5: In him was life; and that life was the light of men, John 1:4.

6: I am the light of the world. Whoever follows me will never walk in darkness, but will have the light of life, John 8:12.

7: If we walk in the light, as he is in the light, we have fellowship with one another, and the blood of Jesus, his Son, purifies us from all sin, 1 John 1:7.

8: Put your trust in the light while you have it, so that you may become [children] of light, John 12:36.

9: You were once darkness, but now you are light in the Lord. Live as children of light, Ephesians 5:8.

10: Let your light shine before men, that they may see your good deeds and praise your Father in heaven, Matthew 5:16.

(Carriers and dancers are all in the sanctuary positioned at director's discretion. Lights may come up for a hymn or the above may be followed by prayer while the sanctuary is lit only by the candles. Congregation can sing a hymn of light, such as "Be Thou My Vision"; "Christ, Whose Glory Fills the Skies"; "Christ Is the World's Light.")

PSALM 104:31-35

Psalm of Praise

PARTICIPANTS: Three or more dancers; one or more readers; or dancers can memorize lines and recite them as they move.

PRESENTATION

Dancers enter before psalm recitation with a three-step turn, left-right-left. Then step forward with right foot, left leg extended behind, arms up above head, palms angled toward each other and back. Freeze [Position 1, page 117].

May the glory of the LORD endure forever.

Repeat three-step turn, left-right-left. Step forward with right foot, arms up, hands same as before.

may the LORD rejoice in his works—

Step back, bringing feet together, bend knees, bring hands down and inward, about abdomen high, palms in. Simultaneously straighten body and circle the palms around each other two to three times as they are raised to chest high. Continue to raise hands up to above head, ending with hands parallel, about twelve inches apart and palms in [Position 2, page 117].

he who looks at the earth, and it trembles,

Bring feet together and lunge left, head down, right leg straight. Extend left arm with palm down, bringing right hand, palm down close to chest. Both hands shake [Position 3, page 118].

who touches the mountains, and they smoke.

Bring right leg to left, rising onto balls of feet, heels off floor, arms above head, hands in prayer position. Quickly lunge forward with right foot. Upper torso is turned to face front; arms come down straight, right is in front of body, left extended out from left side. Both palms down [Position 4, page 118].

I will sing to the LORD all my life;

Three-step turn so that all dancers end in a circle. Some may have to do more than one turn, thereby turning faster than the others or ending the turns with a step or two in order to get into place. They face in.

I will sing praise to my God

Dancers hold hands. Dipping body slightly, they step forward with right foot. Bring all hands up into the center of the circle, left legs extending straight back [Position 5, page 118].

as long as I live.

Dancers rock back on left legs, dipping down slightly again, leaving right legs extended, pointing into circle. Arms swing down and up as bodies and heads lean back, and dancers look straight up [Position 6, page 118].

May my meditation be pleasing to him,
as I rejoice in the LORD.

Release hands of adjacent dancers. Bring right foot back, touch next to left foot, and move it backward to kneel on right knee, at same time bending elbows and lowering arms to shoulder level. In kneeling position, elbows are bent, hands flattened, palms up. Head is up, eyes up, rejoicing in the Lord [Position 7, page 118].

But may sinners vanish from the earth
and the wicked be no more.

Dancers rise and run between and around each other, stopping suddenly in a line, facing forward. They throw arms out straight to sides on "wicked no more" so that each arm crosses that of another dancer at mid-forearm. Palms are forward, legs apart. They will look like they are stopping someone from running through their line.

Praise the LORD,

On "praise" bring feet together. Bring right hand, palm down, in to silently clap the left hand, which is palm up, chest high; and raise both arms, shaking hands body width apart, bending elbows, palms facing each other about shoulder high [Position 8, page 118].

O my soul.

Bring both hands into heart, fingers overlapping, and sweep immediately out and up, palms remain up, fingers

still overlapping a little. Palms will end up facing back with straight arms [Position 9, page 118].
Praise the LORD.
Sweep arms open.

MARY/ANGEL DANCE

Partially Choreographed Advent Dance

SCRIPTURE: Luke 1:26-38
MUSIC: Classical, contemporary, or flute accompaniment.
OPTIONAL READINGS: (1) A poetic introduction to Mary as a young girl read immediately before Mary's entrance. (2) Reading of Luke 1:26-38 any time prior to movement.
PARTICIPANTS: One female as Mary, male (preferable) or female as angel. One or two readers.
COSTUMES: Mary in bright colors, full skirt or dress, ribbons in the hair or dangling from skirt waistband. Looks girlish. Angel in white and/or gold.
PROPS: Bouquet of wildflowers, artificial, or if fresh, artificial used for rehearsals.
DIRECTOR'S NOTE: *Some movement is left to the creativity of the dancer. The early part of the dance, Mary as a carefree young girl, is best done as improvisational or at least without apparent structure.*

READ BEFORE MARY MOVEMENT:

Mary. The Saint. The Virgin. The Pure and Holy. Was she not a child once? An adolescent, happy and carefree? Was she not in love once, with Joseph, maybe. Picking flowers in a meadow for him. Thinking of him.

Dreamy and giddy and young is this Mary we never hear about. She meets God— an angel, a messenger— and gives up her girlishness in an instant. She is a woman now, a woman with a world-changing mission.

Later, when it had begun and she was the center of it all, we wonder if she ever sat quietly by the lake on a tender spring day, a bouquet of freshly picked flowers in her hand, and longed for the days when she was a carefree child.

PRESENTATION

1. **Mary** enters carrying a bouquet of wildflowers. She moves as a young, carefree girl with romance on her mind, with a step-together-step walk or step-touch, step-touch or a skip, depending on the music.

2. **She** stops, extends the right leg forward and to the side, toe pointed, heel up, and keeping legs straight, leans over to pick an imaginary flower with her right hand. She holds the bouquet of flowers above her head in the left hand [Position 1, page 118]. She mimes inserting the picked flower into the bouquet, takes a step, and repeats the flower picking movement on the other side.

3. (a) **She** continues to move about as if walking in a field of flowers on a glorious day. (b) She twirls in an open, carefree manner a couple of times one way, a couple of times the other. (c) She runs and leaps, runs and leaps. She skips, even hops. (d) Now and then she stops to smell the bouquet. (e) She twirls in place, gazing at the sky above her.

4. At the end of the above series of movements, **Mary** runs or skips a few steps and executes a couple of three-step turns.

5. Enter **Angel** during these turns. The angel begins with arms at his [her] sides, a couple of inches away from the body, palms forward. As he [she] steps regally toward Mary, the arms slowly come up until they are above the head in V position, straight arms.

6. Meanwhile, **Mary** is dancing, oblivious to this approaching angel. She is carrying the flowers above her

head in one hand. Either during one of the turns or when she has completed them or when she starts running or skipping forward again, she spots the angel. She comes to an abrupt halt, dropping the flowers in shock at the same time. (This dropping of the flowers signifies real shock and fear in the minds of those watching, so it should be done with the hand raised high in the air so that it is obvious. Flowers should be dropped so that they fall where they won't be in the way of further movement.)

7. **Mary** backs up a couple of steps as the **angel** approaches. Her arms, bent at elbows, extend toward angel, palms out, one above the other in front of face as if to prevent the angel's brightness from blinding her. She is looking to the side, away from the angel [Position 2, page 118].

8. **Angel** drops arms from above head, extends them toward Mary, palms up, fingers slightly curled in as if motioning her to him [her]. **Mary** stops backing up at this sign, but does not drop hands; continues to look to the side, over her own shoulder and down.

9. **Angel** takes Mary's hands and forms them into prayer hands between his [her] own prayer hands. **Mary** does not look at the angel.

10. **Angel** releases her hands and Mary's arms drop to her sides. The angel gently cups her chin in one hand, moves her head so that she is facing him [her], and lifts her head so that she looks into his [her] eyes.

11. The **angel** drops his [her] hands to Mary's shoulders, moves them down her arms to her hands. With her hands in his [hers], the angel raises her arms and turns her so that she has her back to him [her]. Still holding her hands, the angel's arms are now laying over her shoulders while hers are crossed over her chest. They still hold hands.

12. **Angel** and **Mary** sway left then right in this position, then the **Angel** turns her back to where she was facing him [her]. The angel then leads her to a central spot in the front of the sanctuary

13. The **angel** releases her hand and gestures that she

should kneel, which she does on both knees in upright position, arms to her sides, eyes fixed on the angel.

14. The **angel** then dances the message God has for her. (1) Movement to indicate, "The Lord is with you" (within and around you). Lift up arms to designate God and draw down, backs of fingers together loosely, making a line down the center of the body from head to chest area. Head and eyes follow hands [Position 3 Series, page 119].
(2) Movement to indicate, "You have found favor with God or you are holy." Arms spread out from chest area, sweep wide slowly and gracefully to front of body. Eyes on the other dancer [Position 4, page 119].
(3) "You will be with child." Bring hands in to within a few inches of abdomen, cupping them loosely to indicate pregnancy. Head and eyes follow hands [Position 5, page 119].
(4) "You will give birth to Jesus, the great and holy king who will reign forever." Hands move up from abdomen to waist high, cradling a baby. Continue to move arms to chest high, crossed at wrists, palms back, then separate to parallel position and raise above head palms back. Head up, eyes to heavens [Position 6 Series, page 119]. Each position is held for maybe a half a second and moves gracefully into the next, like one movement done in slow motion.

15. **Angel** drops arms and extends a hand to Mary, who rises. Angel backs up a couple of steps, gently leading Mary to where he [she] was standing. The angel drops to one knee, one arm extended up and back, the other arm extended toward Mary [Position 7, page 119].

16. **Mary** repeats the exact motions just completed by the angel to show that she understands and accepts the message. (See above directions for angel.)

17. From the final position, with her arms extended high, **Mary** lunges toward the angel, bring one hand down to grasp the one the angel has extended toward her so that the angel is connected to Mary and God, and Mary is connected to the angel and God [Position 8, page 119].

18. The **angel** loosens his [her] grip and slowly backs

away from Mary. Both dancers keep their hands out-stretched toward each other as if they hate to part. After a few steps, the angel turns and walks out.

19. **Mary** either slowly follows, slowly moves off in another direction, remains in position, or drops to knees in prayer, or other conclusion as suits the director and dancer.

SOLDIERS' DANCE
THE MOCKING OF JESUS

Good Friday Movement

(May be used with the drama as part of Good Friday service. See chapter 5, page 177.)

SCRIPTURE: Matthew 27:27-31, Mark 15:16-20

MUSIC: Solemn classical or new age, a hymn such as "O Sacred Head" or a rhythmic drum beat.

PRESENTERS: Six to eight

PROPS: Spear; a heavy stick; whip; three yards of purple fabric, two to three feet wide; crown of thorns made of grapevine wound in to a crown.

COSTUMES: Dark pants (light-weight warm-ups work well). Dark long-sleeved tops. Gray or black tops may be made from one yard to two yards of polyester with a center hole cut for the head. Jesus may wear a white robe or off-knee length muslin with center cut for the head.

DIRECTOR'S NOTE: *"O Sacred Head," played by piano and violin, can be used as the music for this piece. The dance is a suitable follow-up to the reading of the scripture. The dancers representing any of the roles may be either male or female but are referred to as male for simplicity.*

The director is free to decide where the soldiers are placed or how and when they enter in order to interfere with the progress of Jesus and the spear soldier. Time the soldiers' movements so that they enter and approach the center of the sanctuary at just the right moment to encounter Jesus without Jesus having to alter his pace.

A traditional sanctuary might call for having all participants in place before the movement; they then freeze in position until the moment they encounter Jesus. The spear soldier might force Jesus down the long central aisle to be met by the rod soldier at the first pew, by the whip soldier a few feet further and so on. Jesus could also enter from a door at the front of the sanctuary and commence his walk back and forth or in a large oval in the chancel area.

Since the spear soldiers, rod soldier, robe soldiers, crown soldier, and Jesus all begin the movement with different choreography, it is helpful at the first rehearsal for someone to read aloud each dancer's part while he or she moves through it with the director watching and offering assistance. Rehearse each dancer separately until all dance together.

PRESENTATION

Jesus and Spear Soldier: Jesus enters followed by a soldier who carries a spear. They move slowly into the sanctuary and are intercepted. If there is a long distance to cover, Jesus can falter or stagger and be forced onward by spear soldier.

Enter Rod Soldier:

1. **Soldier** carrying a heavy stick steps sharply in front of and facing Jesus.

2. **Soldier** slams the rod into the open fist of the opposite hand in a typical threatening gesture. Jesus and spear soldier come to abrupt stop.

3. **Rod Soldier** brings rod up chest high holding both ends in hands and steps forward toward Jesus, thrusting the rod toward Jesus. **Jesus** takes one step backward.

4. **Rod Soldier** takes two steps backward and one forward, thrusting the rod toward Jesus on the forward step, while **Jesus** takes two steps forward and one back with each thrust.

5. Repeat sequence for a total of four steps backward for Rod Soldier and forward for Jesus and Spear Soldier. **Spear Soldier** may jab (carefully) Jesus in the back with the spear each time he moves forward.

6. **Rod Soldier** swings to the side doing a three-step turn. If stepping to the right side of Jesus, Rod Soldier steps back and sideways with the right foot, back and sideways with left, and front with right foot. If stepping to the left side, step back and sideways first with the left foot and follow the sequence.

7. **Rod Soldier** brings rod up to shoulder like a rifle at a parade ground as Jesus and Spear Soldier pass, at which point Rod Soldier either steps in beside the Spear Soldier or behind Jesus.

Enter Whip Soldier:

1-4. **Whip Soldier** steps in front of Jesus and stops him, performing the same sequence as the Rod Soldier.

5. After the second set of backward steps, the **Whip Soldier** spins around and walks forward, leading the procession to the front and center of the presentation area. The Rod and Spear Soldiers continue walking to a designated position where they will strike a pose out of the way of the next action.

6. **Whip Soldier** turns to face Jesus, smacking the whip into the fist of the hand not holding it.

7. **Whip Soldier** does a three-step turn, left-right-left.

8. **Whip Soldier** brings right foot in to left and smacks the whip into his hand again.

9. **Whip Soldier** steps back on right foot while bringing whip back; then forward on left; then lunges forward on right, bringing the whip crashing down next to Jesus on the audience side. This is all one continuous whipping motion.

10. **Whip Soldier** steps back two steps, turns sharply, and with back to congregation, walks away, dragging the whip behind him [her] to take place with Rod and Spear Soldier.

Jesus combination in relationship to whip soldier:

1. **Jesus** follows the Whip Soldier with the two-steps-forward-one-back combination, repeating sequence twice.

2. **Jesus** follows Whip Soldier at a distance of several feet to allow for the whipping action.

3. **Jesus** stops walking when Whip Soldier turns and faces him, cracking whip into palm of free hand. (See Whip Soldier instruction 6.)

4. As Whip Soldier turns and prepares to bring the whip down, **Jesus** extends hands forward, palms up, elbows bent in a supplicating movement.

5. As whip is drawn back and brought down, **Jesus** lunges back onto one foot, and looks away from whip sharply, protecting face with hands, palms out. His face should be turned toward the congregation. Thus, if the congregation is sitting to his left, the whip will come down to the floor on his left; and he will step back on the left foot and turn his head as far to the left as he can.

6. **Jesus** returns to standing position with hands extended, palms up as Robe Soldiers approach.

Enter Robe Soldiers:

1. **Robe Soldiers** enter with **Whip Soldier** from opposite sides of the sanctuary or may be in place from the start of the dance but begin moving when the Whip Soldier begins moving. One carries a long purple cloth that symbolizes the robe Jesus was mocked with, draped over both arms.

2. When they reach the presentation area, they remain frozen until whipping has been completed and Whip Soldier turns to walk away.

3. **Robe Soldiers** each grasp an end of the fabric and

together they wrap the cloth around Jesus' waist one full time.

4. They back away from Jesus on either side.

5. **Robe Soldier** with the longest end gives the fabric a tug, and Jesus spins toward that dancer; the next **Robe Soldier** gives her end a tug, and Jesus spins toward the second dancer.

6. In this way, they tug him from side to side several times.

7. **Robe Soldiers** both release the scarf suddenly, appearing to cause Jesus to fall to the floor.

8. **Robe Soldiers** then drag Jesus back to the center of the presentation area.

9. With him there on his knees, they ceremoniously drape the purple cloth over his shoulders like a king's robe.

All Soldiers and Jesus

1. The **Robe Soldiers** are joined by the **Rod, Spear, and Whip Soldiers** who surround **Jesus** in a tight circle. All but **Jesus** bend one arm with fist near shoulder; the other arm pumps up and down in sharp threatening motions. If the Soldier carries a weapon, the weapon will be clutched in the hand pumping. If not, the hand pumping will be in a tight fist. Up and down motions should be done randomly by the dancers, not simultaneously. Do this fairly rapidly and repeatedly three to five times for each person [Position 1, page 119].

2. In the center of the circle, **Jesus** rises slowly up from knees, arms straight up above his head, hands come together into prayer.

3. When he is fully standing with arms completely extended, the **soldiers** freeze wherever their arms happen to be. **Jesus** brings his arms down, right forward, left back at an angle, to waist high, palms down as if blessing those dancers nearest the forward arm [Position 2, page 119].

4. **Jesus** looks at **Soldiers** with love as he does this, and they back away and fall to one knee, heads bowed. He

brings arms back up and repeats the movement with the left arm forward. And those dancers on the left side back away and fall to one knee.

5. Immediately after the last set of **Soldiers** fall to one knee, all rise quickly and rush forward into a lunge toward Jesus, arms stretched toward him, fingers splayed. They shake their arms and fingers as rapidly as possible as they rush him. They back up and rush him again. While they rush him, **Jesus** has arms extended heavenward, both elbows slightly bent, hands cupped to receive, head and eyes up [Position 3, page 120].

6. The **Soldiers** run around Jesus, pressing in close to him, continuing to shake their hands while **Jesus** remains frozen in previous position.

7. The **Soldiers** back away after circling once, opening at center so that congregation can see Jesus. The inside arm as they open up and back around into position is outstretched toward Jesus. The other arm is bent with the hand above the shoulder about ear level, palm facing the head [Position 4, page 120].

8. From behind, a **soldier** places the crown of thorns on Jesus' head. Two others take each of Jesus' hands and lift his arms into the cross position, as if nailing his hands on a cross.

9. When they back away, **Jesus** drops his head backward, or forward, whichever suits the director, and lets his hands dangle lifelessly from the cross position. The **Soldiers** bring their hands up in front of their eyes as if they can't stand to watch his suffering but can't turn away either. The palms face forward with fingers slightly apart [Position 5, page 120].

10. **Jesus** slowly turns to the right and faces each **Soldier**. He brings the fingers of both hands to his lips, and extends his hands, palms down, as if placing a blessing on the head of each dancer in a gentle, forgiving gesture [Position 6, page 120].

11. As **Jesus** gestures to each soldier standing in a semi-

circle around him, that **Soldier** lunges back on the foot nearest the audience, turning body and head away from Jesus and looking down. Arms are down at sides, slightly back, palms facing backward [Position 7, page 120].

12. When **Jesus** has finished the turn and forgiven them all, he trudges out of the sanctuary, bent forward with hands positioned as if he carried the cross on his back, taking slow, plodding steps [Position 8, page 120].

13. One by one, at random, the **Soldiers** turn and face the back of the sanctuary as Jesus departs, and then they too leave by another exit.

SYMBOLS

Good Friday Movement

(May accompany a Good Friday drama and Soldiers Dance)

SCRIPTURE: Matthew 27:11-55, Mark 15:1-40; Luke 22:66—23:49; John 18:28-40, 19:28-30

PRESENTERS: Seven to nine dancers

PROPS: Dark cloth to cover table or altar, spear, rod, whip, purple robe/fabric, crown.

MUSIC: Solemn classical, single-instrument accompaniment, such as flute, violin, or cello, or contemporary, using a hymn such as "What Wondrous Love Is This" or drum beats.

DIRECTOR'S NOTE: *When this movement is a part of a Good Friday drama, the symbol placers can be dancers dressed in mourning black. The following illustrates one way of placing the symbols, but directors are encouraged to present the movement in a manner appropriate to their setting and worship service.*

PRESENTATION

Procession of carriers may enter all at once from different places or one after the other in a procession down one aisle. The symbols may be placed on an altar or communion table. If possible, symbols should be placed from the side of the table rather than from the front so that the congregation can see what is happening.

1. First to come in are the **Spear Carriers**. They precede Cloth Carriers and form an arch under which these people pass. They then take a stance like guards on either side of the communion table or altar where symbols are to be placed.

2. **Cloth Carriers** proceed to drape the altar, communion table and rails, cross, and anything director desires with black drape.

3. **Whip Carrier** enters. The whip is carried or dragged. Whip is placed on the prearranged surface. Carrier backs away from surface with arms extended somewhat, palms out with bent wrists as if warding off the horrors of the whip. He takes a position where congregation can see him as well as the next carriers when they make their placements. Freezes

4. **Rod Carrier** enters raising rod with one hand on each end and lowering with every other step or so. Places rod on table, and with elbows bent, crosses arms at forehead level and turns head as if warding off blows from a rod to the head. Freezes.

5. Enter **Carrier with a purple cloth**, representing the robe with which Jesus was mocked. Cloth is draped over hands which are held about shoulder high and body-width apart, elbows bent. Cloth is allowed to hang low in front. At the table or altar, carrier clutches a wad of the cloth in each hand. He or she brings the right hand in to chest and out, then the same with the left hand. He or she then brings both hands into the center of the chest clutching the

cloth in the fists and approaches the table this way [Position 1, page 120].

6. He or she carefully drapes the cloth, then bows the head and folds hands in prayer, takes his or her position, and freezes.

7. The **Crown Carrier** enters with a crown of thorns. At the table, he or she raises the crown above the head and sways in a circle from the waist as if feeling faint [Position 2 Series, page 120].

8. He or she lifts crown forward as an offering to the cross, holds momentarily, then places the crown on the table. Stepping forward on one foot, he or she raises hands, palms facing each other, fingers tense and splayed and curled slightly as if clutching the feet of Christ to pull him down [Position 3, page 120].

9. **Spear Carrier(s)** moves from position, brings the spear to the table, and lays it with the other symbols. Carrier backs away, turns to face congregation, front and center, and bows head.

10. A **Grieving Woman** rushes toward the table where the others are gathered. Before arriving, she pivots sharply and turns to run in another direction. She runs a few steps, pivots again and rushes in another direction. She looks frantic and in shock, as if she doesn't know where to go or what to do. Each turn to go in the opposite direction should be sharp and follow very sudden stops.

11. The **Grieving Woman** is stopped by a **Spear Carrier** when she is just beyond arm's length. The spear carrier lunges forward with the left arm up, palm forward to stop the running woman.

12. She stops and slowly brings up her right hand to place her right palm against the left palm of the spear carrier. Each takes a step forward with the back leg so that they are standing straight and closer together. Each brings the other hand up to match flattened palms [Position 4, page 120].

13. They curl fingers, intertwining them and lower their arms, fingers still entwined. They lean toward each other,

taking a small step forward and to the side. Still holding hands, they lean toward each other so that the right shoulder of one is touching the right shoulder of the other. Repeat on the other side [Position 5, page 120].

14. The **Spear Carrier** releases his or her grip and places an arm around the shoulder of the **Grieving Woman,** escorting her to join the others who form a semicircle around the symbol table, or if that's not possible, in a circle in front of the table.

Altar or Circle Movements:

15. Holding hands, all dancers sway right, then left, leading with the shoulder, letting the head follow. Repeat.

16. They do a three-step turn to the right, then a three-step turn left.

17. Their right feet pull in to the left as the arms are raised up toward a real or visualized cross.

18. Dancers slowly drop straight arms down at sides to shoulder level, palms facing forward and stop in the position of a cross. They sharply bend the wrists and let the hands drop loosely, as if life has gone out of them. Palms should still be turned partially forward as they dangle downward. Their heads fall forward abruptly, again as if life has gone out of the body. They hold this lifeless position for a second.

19. They begin sinking to the knees by letting the body curl in on itself. The whole process should look as if the sudden weight of what has happened is too much to bear, forcing the sufferers to their knees.

20. On their knees, arms bent at the elbows with hands coming forward in front of the face, their arms are parallel and about six inches apart. Their heads are bowed [Position 6, page 120].

21. **Carriers** may remain frozen on knees with heads bowed as lights are dimmed and service ends; or they may rise and process out with heads bowed, arms loosely at sides or around each other. Some of the carriers may want to look back at the scene in sorrow and then exit.

EASTER MOVEMENT WITH RECITATION

Choreographed Scripture Interpretation

PARTICIPANTS: Two or more dancers representing the women at the tomb and three speakers, a narrator and two angels, or one doing all parts.

SCRIPTURE: Luke 24:1-8

COSTUMES: Narrator in street clothes. Angels, especially if reading, may also be in street clothes, or wear white or gold tops with white pants or skirts. During the narration, dancers either wear black or wrap black stoles about their shoulders, covering as much of the colorful clothing underneath as possible. If the dancers are to reappear in costume, these drapes can be quickly thrown off.

PROPS: Containers for spices that some or all of the women carry. Pieces of black cloth to cover Easter morning symbols, such as flowers, plants, altar, cross, communion table, and so forth. Optional cross and/or large object made to look like a boulder, banner(s), or colorful scarves if dancers are to be part of the choir processional.

SUGGESTED SETTING AND LIGHTS: If possible, lighting should be dim when people enter the sanctuary and raised a little at a time when angels announce that he has risen.

MUSIC: Solemn Instrumental, drum beat.

DIRECTOR NOTES: *This movement/drama may be used as a dramatic introduction to "Lift High the Cross" or similar anthem, either as processional or as dance. Dancers may precede or follow the choir, carrying banners and/or a cross or whirling long, colorful scarves.*

*When the service is begun with dim lighting and solemn pre-
lude music and everything is covered in black, most people are
startled. They are forced to think about what the first Easter
morning must have really been like—that for the women and the
disciples, Jesus was dead and they were in mourning. As a result,
when the angels appear and the dancers start coming to life, so
does the congregation. The removal of the black coverings and the
raising of the lights to allow the color and brightness to appear is
very dramatic and long remembered. This is especially true if the
movement and drama is followed by an Easter dance.*

PRESENTATION

The Narrator reads all the lines indicated until the angels
enter. The Narrator may want to wait before reading the
first lines until the dancers have begun entering the sanctuary, depending on how far they have to walk to arrive at
their destination.

**Narrator: On the first day of the week, very early in
the morning, the women took the spices they had
prepared and went to the tomb.**

1. Enter **dancers**, moving slowly and solemnly. Two or
three are carrying vessels containing spices, two might be
walking with arms around each other for comfort, one
might carry a cloth for wiping eyes or be otherwise weep-
ing, one might be walking in a state of shock, eyes focused
straight ahead, seemingly oblivious to the others. A cross in
plain view can be stared at with the disbelief or horror one
might expect seeing the execution device of one we love.
Perhaps one of the dancers stares at the cross and looks
away in agony. All the time, the dancers are moving
toward a specified area which may be an altar or a kneeling rail or the foot of a cross or just the upper portion of the
chancel. The dancers should stop in a formation that allows
the congregation to see their movements. For example,
they may stand in an A formation at the foot of a cross.

Narrator: They found the stone rolled away from the tomb, but when they entered, they did not find the body of the Lord Jesus.

2. **Spice Carriers**, arriving at their destination first, set the spices down. All bring hands up about chest high, back to back, and thrust them forward and apart as if parting a curtain. They continue parting their arms to form a V in front of their body, about waist high. At *"they did not find"* their palms, which are now facing backward, flip up, right palm, then left in an "I-don't-understand-this" gesture. Their heads should turn and look at the hand that is being flipped over [Position 1 Series, page 121].

Narrator: While they were wondering about this, suddenly two men in clothes that gleamed like lightning stood beside them.

3. The **angels** appear suddenly. The **women** see one or all of them with sharp looks in their direction, and fall to both knees, sitting back on heels.

Narrator: In their fright the women bowed down with their faces to the ground, but the men said to them:

4. From full kneeling position, the women lean over with face almost touching the floor.

Angel 1: Why do you look for the living among the dead? He is not here; He has risen!

5. From full kneeling positions, the women raise their upper body, sitting back on heels, to look at the speaking angel [Position 2, page 121].

Angel 2: Remember how he told you, while he was still with you in Galilee:

6. The women straighten bodies from knees [Position 3, page 121].

Angel 2: The Son of Man must be delivered into the hands of sinful men, be crucified, and on the third day be raised again.

7. The women rise to feet, still looking at speaking angel, arms at sides.

Angel 1: He has risen.

8. The angels dip body, scooping hands in from sides to front, elbows bent, parallel about eight inches apart, palms in, tips of fingers about head high. Their eyes should look up [Position 4, page 121].

Angel 2: The cross is now a banner.

9. The angels raise hands up and out into cross position, palms forward.

Angel 1: Lift it high in triumph.

10. The angels dip body and scoop hands down and up, palms up as if lifting a plate on each hand [Position 5, page 121].

Angel 2: No more shroud of death.

11. Dancers remove a black cover or covers, depending on number of dancers you have and number of items covered and carry to a designated spot to be released.

Angel 1: No more dark despair.

12. Dancers remove a second set of covers and carry away.

Angel 2: No more bleak hopelessness.

13. Dancers remove a third set of covers and carry away.

Angel 1: Lift high the cross, for he has risen.

14. All assume position for dance if there is to be one or freeze in a worshipful position as the choir begins a processional. If there is a cross available to be carried, dancers might lift it and proceed to meet the choir as it enters. Dancers carrying banners, crosses, and colorful scarves may also proceed or follow the choir.

PENTECOST

Scripture Interpretation with Movement

SCRIPTURE: Verses from Acts 2:1-8, 14-37, 38.
PARTICIPANTS: Any number of dancers, the more the better, one speaker to read scripture.
COSTUMES: Suitable colors are the colors of fire: white, red, orange, yellow, royal blue; or all costumes are white with the stoles in the Pentecost colors.
PROPS: Fabric four to six inches wide (or wider) and two yards long, made of flowing material. Material is to be bunched together on the shoulders.
DIRECTOR'S NOTE: *The reader should be expressive with a commanding voice. He or she should rehearse with the dancers often in order to know how to pace the reading and to pause when necessary. It is also possible for the dancer playing Peter to speak Peter's lines.*

PRESENTATION

(Adapted from choreography by Mary Bell)

1. When the day of Pentecost came, they were all together in one place.
Dancers enter in group formation of an *A* or *triangle*, if possible from several entrances into the sanctuary. Their arms are straight and spread out at 45 degree angles from the body, palms forward, fingers toward the ground. If there are enough dancers, their arms may cross another dancer's arm between wrist and elbow.
2. Suddenly a sound like the blowing of a violent wind came from heaven and filled the whole house where they were sitting.
Dancers run very fast, arms extended behind them, palms down, like airplane wings to end up at a central spot in a semicircle or circle formation. If all dancers enter from one place, they will run in a large circle.

3. They saw what seemed to be tongues of fire that separated and came to rest on each of them.

One by one in a ripple effect, each dancer removes strip of fabric from own shoulders and places over the head to rest on the shoulders of person in front of him or her so that middle of the fabric is draped loosely over the upper chest and the ends are dangling down the back. Heads of the recipients are bowed to allow this to occur.

4. All of them were filled with the Holy Spirit and began to speak in other tongues as the Spirit enabled them.

All sharply lift heads and turn heads only to face congregation. Each person begins speaking at the same time, the mouth moving distinctly but the voice should begin very low, possibly while reader is reading the scripture. The volume of voices increases and then lowers to a murmur again. The following are suggestions but other languages can be added, or replace any of the statements. The idea is to say something about the Spirit of God or about Jesus in another tongue.

Dancers A: The Holy Spirit is upon us.

Dancers B: *Veni Sancte Spiritus.* (Latin: Come Holy Spirit.)

Dancers C: *Jesus perdona el pecados.* (Spanish: Jesus pardons sin.)

Dancers D: *In Gott ist sta'rke und freiheit.* (German: In God is strength, power, and freedom.)

5. Now there were staying in Jerusalem God-fearing Jews from every nation under heaven.

Dancers move from their places to another place, some criss-crossing the circle and moving past each other, others move out and away; they should move sharply, with bold, rhythmic steps.

6. When they heard this sound, a crowd came together in bewilderment, because each one heard them speaking in his own language.

The dancers continue walking from verse 5 into 6, coming together in "crowd" formation (as suits the director), with each dancer striking a pose that depicts awe, amazement, fear, any emotion your group considers appropriate under the circumstances. They freeze in this pose.

7. Utterly amazed, they asked: "Are not all these men who are speaking Galileans? Then how is it that each of us hears them in his own native language?"

Dancers move quickly so that they are in an A formation, loosely formed. Each dancer switches from original pose to one of the other poses, all at the same time or randomly as suits the director.

8. Peter's response was to review the prophecies of the prophet Joel and to tell the story of Jesus' life among them.

One dancer, playing Peter, moves from the group and continues in a wide sweep, looking at the congregation and gesturing in teacher-like fashion: Cross arms chest high, fingertips resting lightly on opposite upper arms. Keeping elbows bent, lift first one arm, extending index finger straight up, then the other, looking at the audience all the while. Peter takes a position in the center and in back of the rest of the dancers [Position 1 Series, page 121].

9. The crowd asked, "What then should we do?"

Except for Peter-dancer, dancers all fall to knees, arms parallel in front of body, palms up, one hand slightly behind the other, elbows bent. Peter-dancer remains standing, arms bent at elbows and in front about body width apart, palms up.

10. Peter replied, "Repent and be baptized, every one of you, in the name of Jesus Christ, for the forgiveness of your sins.

Peter-dancer spreads hands, palms down, from center position outward to either side and in front, about waist high as if blessing the group in front of him or her. The other dancers pull hands into prayer position at chest and bow heads in humility. This can be done in unison or with a ripple effect starting with those nearest the Peter-dancer.

11. And you will receive the gift of the Holy Spirit."

Dancers lift heads. Prayer hands are raised in front of body, head high, with elbows bent. Separate hands about two inches apart and cup hands slightly, bending at the wrists, as if to catch a basketball-size Holy Spirit [Position 2, page 121].

DANCE POSITIONS

SPIRIT OF THE LIVING GOD

Position 1

Position 2

PSALM 104

Position 1

Position 2

Position 3

Position 4

Position 5

Position 6

Position 7

Position 8

Position 9

MARY/ANGEL DANCE

Position 1

Position 2

Position 3 Series

Position 4

Position 5 and 6 Series

Position 7

Position 8

SOLDIER'S DANCE

Position 1

Position 2

A   B

Position 3

Position 4

Position 5

Position 6

Position 7

Position 8

SYMBOLS

Position 1

Position 2 Series

Position 3

Position 4

Position 5

Position 6

EASTER MOVEMENT

Position 1 Series

Position 2

Position 3

Position 5

Position 4

PENTECOST

Position 1 Series

Position 2

Chapter Four

GOD'S MESSENGER
The Clown as Minister

We are fools for Christ.
1 Corinthians 4:10

The clown as minister differs from the circus clown in one major aspect. The circus or party clown is present primarily to entertain, though there may be a message in the clown's program, while the ministering clown is present to share the gospel, nearly always entertaining as well.

An ideal minister, the clown catches and holds our attention if for no other reason than the way he or she looks. With the bright colors, mismatched clothing, wild hair, bizarre hat, exaggerated expressions, and face paint, who is going to look elsewhere?

Now that he has our attention, he teaches us a lesson, and we learn it because we don't know we are being taught. Our defenses are down, and we are vulnerable to ideas because we think we are just being entertained. What do clowns teach us with their crazy antics? Fumbles approaches a heavy obstacle. She tries all sorts of tactics to remove it so that she can be on her way, never once considering that she could simply go around it. Isn't this what we do sometimes? We try everything under the sun to solve a problem except the most obvious solution. Clowns help us to look at our own foolishness with gentle humor rather than with shame and anger.

Clowns approach complex ideas with the simplicity of a child, drawing our attention to when we are doing likewise. To a clown, building a church means just that—providing a structure with brick and mortar. Adults know that Christ's church consists of people doing good works, but do we sometimes find we are distracted from that purpose by concerns for the structure in which we meet? Clowns show us where we have wandered from our path and gently nudge us back to the journey toward God.

Often, while we are learning the lessons a clown teaches, we are laughing. Laughter makes us vulnerable to new ideas, heals our inner wounds, and releases our tension. We are energized by humor; our health improved. The clown makes our mistakes less important, our tragedies more bearable, our pain less hurtful.

In light of all this, it is easy to see that clowning belongs in the worship setting. But when, where, and how do you bring clowns into the sanctuary on Sunday morning without people thinking they are in a circus arena instead of church?

WHEN TO BRING IN THE CLOWNS

You bring in the clowns when the scripture or theme of the service is conducive to clowning. Clowns can set a mood for worship, entering early in the service, possibly with the processional. They may hand out flowers to the women on Mother's Day, toss pieces of crepe paper like confetti in a New York parade on Palm Sunday, or carry banners on Pentecost. Clowns may deliver the children's message, illustrate scripture, or enhance the sermon.

How do you come up with a clown skit that illustrates scripture or a moral? One way is to select a scripture or message and then locate a previously written skit that fits your needs. Or start with the skit and find the appropriate scripture to illustrate it. The skits included at the end of this chapter will get you started. In addition, other resources are listed in appendix B, page 194.

However, if clown skits are to be presented numerous times in worship, you will need to create your own clown sketches, which has the added benefit of nurturing the imagination of the creators.

PREPARING SKITS

Even as clowns prepare to teach, they are learning, for the clown, just as the actor, must understand the story, the message, and the characters that he or she is to illustrate. The process for preparing skits for presentation is the same as that for dramatic scripture or skit presentation. The scripture or skit must be read out loud, followed by an analysis of the plot, character, and message, including a discussion that considers each participant's point of view. After people have clowned a few times and formed their own personas or clown personalities, they and the director will see certain clown personas acting as certain biblical characters almost automatically. Even more than drama and dance, individual creativity is very important in clowning. How to convey a character as a clown, especially through mime, demands much from the often neglected imagination; but with each clown skit, the imagination is rekindled and begins to bloom and grow. The director's job in all this is to allow time for enough repetition and to point out what works and what doesn't.

CREATING SKITS FROM SCRIPTURE

Creating a skit begins by reading the scripture and clearly understanding the message that is to be conveyed, being aware that not all scripture or messages are appropriate for clowning. Look for scripture that tells a story, one with action such as the parables. Or you may want to tell your own story in a way that illustrates a scripture text. For instance, how would you illustrate the message we must love our enemies and do good to those who hate us. As you look at the scripture as story, whether your own or biblical, let yourself imagine either young children or clowns acting it out. In the case of the lost coin parable, for instance, can you see a clown rushing around, looking in strange places for a missing stuffed animal or rock? Visualize a child acting out Daniel in the lion's den or Jonah and the whale? It can be an unnerving learning experience to interpret adult behavior the way a child would. Have you ever witnessed a young child scold a doll or friend and recognized yourself? Did you learn a lesson from that?

CREATE CONTEMPORARY SKITS

Another way to illustrate a message is to take a modern-day situation and present it with the characters and their reactions greatly exaggerated. It is a little frightening how easily we can see ourselves in some of the most absurd portrayals. In "The Carpenter" Frank Fussbudget shakes his fist, stomps his feet, and otherwise throws a clownish temper tantrum over Dalton Disorderly's messy yard and unruly kids and hires a carpenter to build a tall, solid privacy fence as a solution. Many months after doing the skit in worship, I was appalled to see myself acting exactly like Frank Fussbudget when I grumpily demanded my husband build a fence to prevent my having to see a neighbor's untidy yard.

We learn from clowns in the most painless way of all, letting them act out our most ridiculous, even mean-spirited, feelings while hanging on to our self-esteem. Look at a real-life problem, see the story through a child's eyes, and show the story with a clown skit.

GROUP CREATIONS

A director may want to ask the presenters to help create a clown skit, making the presentation that much more meaningful to the persons involved, while lessening the workload of the director.

For example, if a group helped to create the skit "Treasures," which illustrates Matthew 6:19-21, the presenters may consider the things they tend to treasure in their lives, such as computers, stereos, or sports equipment as well as items a child might call a treasure. For a child, the very word *treasure* might conjure up a treasure chest. Thus, when the teacher begins discussing the treasure Jesus is talking about, everyone runs off to fetch treasures, beginning with a treasure chest.

Then the group would consider what treasures in heaven might be, coming up with words not things, such as *love*, *compassion*, *forgiveness*, and *caring*. But how do you show concepts when they aren't tangible? Consider who gives love, compassion, forgiveness, and caring? People do. Therefore, when the clowns are told to gather their treasures, one of the clowns gathers people.

Group creations take more time, but the presenters usually enjoy the creating process, which stimulates imagination and builds pride and self-confidence. In addition, working together through clowning is insightful and just plain fun.

CLOWN CHARACTERIZATION

To be a clown, we must first lose ourselves. The white face of the Christian clown symbolizes the death of the adult self, and the colors symbolize new life, the rebirth of the trusting, accepting, faithful, forgiven child. There is a tremendous sense of freedom in this transformation, allowing an adult to be someone else, someone without gender, age, race, or religion and therefore impeded by none of these.

Moreover, natural shyness does not hinder a person presenting a skit in worship because it is the clown, Sweetfeet or Chili Bean, appearing in front of a congregation, not Linda or Jane. In fact, an adult who is shy might find it relieving to let his or her clown be a shy clown. Being true to self by letting your clown become who you really are inside may reveal to you that your shyness or clumsiness or nervousness is, in fact, very acceptable to others.

Most people love a clown; and while an individual might not feel comfortable showing that love in a verbal or visible way to an actor or a dancer, he or she often will do so with a clown. A hug or handshake from that taciturn church member who never smiles is as beneficial to the clown's self-esteem as to the church member's.

COSTUMES AND MAKEUP

Any good book on clowning will contain details on the basic clown types—white face, august, and tramp—including makeup for each as well as typical costuming. Appendix A includes the steps to creating a clown face with full makeup as suggested by Floyd Shaffer, the founder and leader of clown ministry.

For brief skits in worship, however, I have found that full makeup and costuming are not always necessary. Totally making up the face takes considerable time that most people are not willing to devote on a Sunday morning, particularly for a three-minute skit that takes place in the middle of worship. In addition, specially made clown costumes cost more money than most people want to spend and once made or purchased may not be appropriate for the role being played in the next skit.

In most cases, a red dot on each cheek and/or on the tip of the nose and an outfit made up primarily from a standard wardrobe and/or a trip to a second-hand store constitutes a clown in the eyes of the congregation. Oversized or undersized clothing, mismatched colors and designs, gaudy suspenders or belts, funny hats and hairstyles, and silly slippers or mismatched shoes provided excellent costumes. This way, clown clothing can be changed quickly and red dots removed easily with a dab of baby oil or baby shampoo so that the presenter can join the congregation for the remainder of the worship service.

As laughter is infectious, so is clowning. Clowning tends to bond a group together. Maybe it's the laughter; maybe it's poignancy in a clown's portrayal of love and generosity, of anger and loneliness, or the working together to help each other improve. Whatever it is, clowning together is nothing short of joyful, and clowns always feel better when they leave a rehearsal than they did when they arrived.

SKITS

Presentation tips:
1. Allow approximately one minute for each page of script.
2. Props should be large and distinct so that the congregation can recognize them from a distance.
3. Encourage individual presenters to provide their own props whenever possible.

GIFTS IN THE SCHOOL OF LIFE

Using Our Talents for Others

SCRIPTURE: Matthew 5:5, Matthew 20:26-27,
1 Corinthians 12 (any part or the entire chapter),
Galatians 5:13, Philippians 2:3.
THEME: Humility, meekness, serving, and the value of all gifts, however humble

PRESENTERS: Five miming clowns and one non-clown story-teller.

Mr. Kinder—Teacher (may be Mrs. or Miss)

Milly—Outstanding talent

Shawna—Behind-the-scenes worker

Gretchen—Shy poet

Dobby—Clumsy clown who cooks

Narrator/storyteller

PROPS: GENERAL—5 chairs, table for cooking demonstrations and another desk/table or lectern for teacher, or both characters may use the same table; a sign that says "RECITAL" or "SHOWTIME"; ribbons for the students, each appropriately marked as follows:

Shawna: BEST HELPER or ENCOURAGER or the equivalent.

Gretchen: BEST POET

Dobby: BEST COOK

Milly: BEST MUSICIAN

PROPS FOR INDIVIDUAL CHARACTERS: Mr. Kinder: empty pasta box with long noodle/or string taped to it or other disciplinary tool. Other teaching tools as desired. **Milly:** one or more of the following: horn, drum, child's keyboard or piano, harmonica, any other musical instruments desired. **Shawna:** (optional) cleaning supplies such as a dust rag. **Gretchen:** notebook and pencil. **Dobby:** pitcher for lemonade, rubber chicken, good looking cake, lopsided cake, baking sheet on which there are cookies, paper cups that are hidden beneath the table upon which she prepares her goodies, (optional) cooking utensils that may include a mixing bowl and spoon, measuring cups, saucepan or skillet.

COSTUMES: Milly's costume may include long eyelashes and golden curls or the equivalent adornments to create the "pretty, perfect little girl," clown style. **Dobby** might wear an apron, **Gretchen,** oversized, round glasses or something else that conveys she's smart and artistic.

DIRECTOR'S NOTE: *This skit features narration and no memorization. All narration is mimed as the story unfolds, the more exaggerated the gestures, especially of the recital, the better. Shawna may enter with Narrator or enter beforehand, or enter* *after the story starts. She can be tidying up teacher's desk, sweeping, or some such activity.*

SCENE: Students are sitting in chairs/desks while teacher stands before them.

PRESENTATION

Narrator: I'd like to introduce you to Mr. Kinder and the students in his school of life. As you know, this is a public school, open to everybody. Let me begin with Mr. Kinder. *(Enter **Mr. Kinder** who mimes as the narrator reads.)*

Mr. Kinder is one of those rare teachers who not only inspires learning but truly loves all of his students, treating them fairly and respecting their individuality. He challenges his students, however, to do their best to set and satisfy their own goals, and to reach the height of their capabilities.

Mr. Kinder isn't an easy teacher, and he can and does chastise when necessary. He does this because his students need guidance. They must understand right from wrong and how to live accordingly if they are to feel secure and be happy.

The students love Mr. Kinder, and because they want to give back to him all the love and care he has given them, they decide to present a show, hoping to please him with their talents.

*(**Milly** performs while **Shawna** takes a seat to admire **Milly** as she demonstrates her talents)*

Milly can't wait to start the show. She dances. She sings. She does acrobatics. She even plays the horn, a drum, and a piano. And if she couldn't do a thing, some folks say it wouldn't matter because Milly is beautiful with her luxurious curls, long, thick eyelashes, and perfect figure. People just enjoy looking at Milly. *(Pause)* And nobody enjoys it more than Shawna. She is one of Milly's most ardent admirers.

(**Gretchen.** *She tries to get herself to rise, maybe encouraged by others.*) Gretchen is different altogether from Milly. Not that she doesn't have talent. Gretchen writes beautiful poetry, but Gretchen is afraid. She fears people will laugh at her or mock her or criticize her. The other students want to hear one of her poems at their show, but Gretchen is too shy to read one even though she loves Mr. Kinder. She is convinced he will be disappointed in her, and Gretchen is afraid to take the chance.

As usual, Shawna talks Gretchen into performing. She insists no one will laugh or criticize. "We'll rehearse together," she suggests, and promises to sit in the front row to give support during the show. Reluctantly, Gretchen agrees.

And then there's Dobby.

(**Dobby** *stumbles to her place, dropping items as she goes.* **Shawna** *comes to her aid. Dobby's entire performance is executed with considerable flourish and calamity, none of which bothers Dobby in the slightest. It's Shawna who dashes around to catch falling pots and wipe up spills and stains.*)

Dobby is clumsy, not very smart, and a little on the shy side. She cannot possibly perform for Mr. Kinder, but she can cook. Oh boy, can she cook!

She burns herself a lot and drops things and bumps into things, but she can cook! Somehow her German chocolate cake *[or other kind of cake]* and lemon cookies won first prize at the state fair last year. She baked both for Mr. Kinder's after-show party, and she made her excellent lemonade from scratch. She spilled quite a lot while pouring it into the serving pitcher, but that was all right because Shawna cleaned up the mess.

(**Shawna** *is cleaning up Dobby's mess and perhaps giving Gretchen some last minute instructions on poetry reading.*)

Poor Shawna. Shawna does nothing. She is nice, certainly, but she has no talent whatever. She tries to dance and sing. *(Others might close their ears or shake their heads in sorrow, but no one should laugh at Shawna's efforts.)* But as you can see, it's hopeless. Once she baked a cake, but it fell before she could take it out of the oven. Another time she made chicken and noodles, but the chicken came out so tough it tasted like rubber. *(Dobby might demonstrate a lopsided cake and rubber chicken.)*

All the other students think it is too bad that Shawna has no gift for Mr. Kinder and nothing to contribute to the show or party afterward because they know she really loves the teacher as much as they do.

(Enter someone carrying a sign indicating the party is about to begin and/or a sign indicating that time has passed.)

The day of the show arrives, and it's time for the students to display their gifts.

(Shawna applauds each performer and otherwise offers encouragement.)

Milly is first, of course.

(Milly might play all instruments at once while dancing at the same time to demonstrate her ability and make it different from before.)

Mr. Kinder couldn't be more pleased. He thoroughly enjoys her performance. Mr. Kinder loves Gretchen's poem though he wishes she'd hold her head up and smile. Shawna is coaxed into a brief dance, but it's rather a fiasco and she gives up quickly.

It is after the performance that Dobby demonstrates her talent. She offers Mr. Kinder one of her cookies, and he eats with pure rapture on his face. He would doubtless find her lemonade just as savory except he has no way to drink it.

(Shawna immediately begins to search for the cups.)

Everyone has been too busy putting on the show to remember cups for the lemonade. Mr. Kinder doesn't complain. He thanks Dobby for the cookie anyway. And then he looks around for Shawna.

(**Shawna** *is under the desk, desperately trying to locate the cups, tossing things all over the place, but of course, no one notices at first.*)

Mr. Kinder asks each of the students where Shawna is, but no one knows. "We must look until we find her then," Mr. Kinder tells the students. So they look. And they look and they look

(*Everyone begins to look, peering under and behind things until* **Shawna** *leaps up from the floor triumphantly holding a cup aloft.*)

And then suddenly, Mr. Kinder spots the lost student. "Look! There she is!" He exclaims, delighted. The students greet Shawna with much relief that she is no longer lost.

And now it's time for awards. Mr. Kinder bestows a ribbon upon Milly for best musical performance, upon Dobby for best cook, upon Gretchen for best poet. And then they all look at Shawna. Poor Shawna. What can Mr. Kinder possibly give her an award for?

But Mr. Kinder has no trouble recognizing Shawna's gifts. He gives her the ribbon for best helper, and then he tells them all. "Shawna has earned the most important award of all. For it is Shawna's willingness to give her gifts that allows everybody else to give theirs."

THE CARPENTER

Love Thy Neighbor

SCRIPTURE: Colossians 3:12-14. Also Proverbs 11:12; Matthew 5:44, 7:1.

THEME: Letting Jesus into our lives brings love and acceptance of others.

PRESENTERS: Four miming clowns who speak now and then in memorized dialogue.

Frank Fussbudget—neat, tidy, very precise, organized.

Dalton Disorderly—sloppy, easily distracted, disorganized.

Leroy Disorderly—a child.

The Carpenter—a carpenter/Jesus

Reader/storyteller/narrator

PROPS: A bean bag or child's ball that doesn't bounce.

OPTIONAL PROPS: Two picket fences made from cardboard, two feet long and one foot high. On one fence is printed "DISORDERLY" on the other, "FUSSBUDGET," a real or child's tool chest with various tools for building, such as a hammer. All other props are mimed.

DIRECTOR'S NOTE: *This is a clown skit with dialogue. Because of the memorization and the need for superb timing, the skit requires more than the average number of rehearsals—at least two, preferably three. Also, paying special attention to casting details will help. Consider having someone who is naturally disorderly play Dalton Disorderly, and someone who prefers things tidy to play Fussbudget. Another possibility is to have a carpenter who knows how to use tools play Carpenter, which will allow for a more natural mime of bridge building.*

Ask the clowns to memorize their lines before the first rehearsal. At the first rehearsal run through the skit with the storyteller several times without any action, which gives the storyteller an opportunity to become accustomed to the interruption of the narration and the clowns a chance to work on inflection and tempo. During the second rehearsal, the presenters concentrate on the mime, while the third is used for fine-tuning the timing.

PRESENTATION

Note: *Clowns mime the story as the narrator reads, speaking their lines when indicated.*

Narrator: Frank Fussbudget kept a perfect house with a perfect yard. He pulled weeds every day, watered his lawn twice a week, and fertilized his roses once a month. Frank didn't have a wife to nag him into doing these things; he did them because he liked order. He had no children to complicate things and no pets. He did not even feed the birds because they scattered shells from the seeds, which messed up his perfect lawn.

Frank's nearest neighbor was Dalton Disorderly. Dalton did have a wife, but she was far too busy chasing after six kids to nag him about their yard. Dalton tried to keep the lawn mowed and the hedges trimmed and the weeds pulled, but it seemed he was always interrupted by his Golden Retriever wanting to play or one of the kids tossing him a Frisbee or the birds needing more food. There was always something.

One day little Leroy Disorderly pitched a ball into Frank Fussbudget's yard. This time the offending missile landed within an inch of Frank's prize rosebush. Looking around for the offender, his eyes fell upon a small trespasser. Frank sprang forward and snatched up poor little Leroy.

Leroy: I'm sorry, Sir. I just wanted to get my ball.

Narrator: Before Frank had a chance to explain in detail what he intended to do with that ball and its pitcher, Leroy's father bounded into Frank's yard.

Dalton: Unhand that child!

Narrator: And soon the two men were squabbling and fighting. Among other things, Frank said:

*(**Leroy** dances around encouraging a fight during the next lines.)*

Frank: I have a right to a perfect yard in a quiet, peaceful neighborhood. I have a right to a safe yard to wander in without being bombarded by missiles.

Dalton: I will not imprison my children and inhibit their growth worrying about your yard. A man's home and grounds are meant to be lived in, not admired.

Frank: Oh, yeah?

Dalton: Yeah!

Leroy: Attaboy, Dad.

Frank: Go! Off my property at once!

Dalton: You know what you are? *(pauses to consider something really awful until it dawns on him)* You're the neighborhood grouch, that's what you are.

Narrator: And with that, he grabbed Leroy by the arm and marched him home. *(pause)*

It took a while for Dalton to calm down. He paced. He stomped his feet. He clinched his fist. He paced some more. About that time a stranger, carrying a tool box and some wood under his arm, appeared in the yard.

Carpenter: Good afternoon. I'm a carpenter. I wondered if you might have some work for me today.

Narrator: At first Dalton told him no; but on thinking about it, he decided the answer was yes.

Dalton: I want a fence built.

Narrator: He said and pointed to the side of his back-yard, the side that bordered the perfect yard of Frank Fussbudget.

Dalton: I want the fence made of slats with no spaces between them. I do not want to even look at my neighbor or his perfect yard.

Narrator: Eager for work, the carpenter smilingly agreed. The two men established a fair price to be paid on completion of the job, and the carpenter set to work. Dalton said to himself:

Dalton: I'll paint my side of the fence an attractive bright yellow. I will not paint Fussbudget's side at all. Let the old grouch look at an ugly unpainted fence. That will show him.

Narrator: Show him what, Dalton didn't really know, but he stomped away to buy his yellow paint. While he was gone, the carpenter, humming happily to himself, hammered together wooden boards. He was an expert, an artist. He was also fast, efficient, and knowledgeable. There was no question watching him work that he not only loved his job but knew precisely what he was doing *(pause)*. But wait! What's this? Did he know what he was doing? That wasn't a fence he had constructed. No, it wasn't a fence at all. It was ... why ... the carpenter had built a bridge.

Clearly satisfied with his work, the carpenter began to gather his tools. He didn't get very far before Dalton arrived with paint in hand. On seeing the carpenter's work, he was, at first, perplexed. And then, furious.

Dalton: Why you fool! Don't you know the difference between a fence and a bridge?

Narrator: He shook his fist at the carpenter in fury, demanding he pull apart the bridge and build his fence as promised.

Just then, Frank Fussbudget appeared in his yard. He spotted the bridge, of course, and was startled; but he couldn't help admiring it. No one appreciated beauty more than Frank. Still, Frank being a practical man, knew a bridge was built to allow passage over some obstacle, and there was no obstacle. Or was there? Of course, it had to be. The only obstacle was the misunderstanding between himself and Dalton.

Frank: The bridge must be Dalton's effort to reconcile. A rather odd effort, but clever. Yes, very clever.

Narrator: After picking a flower from his prize rosebush, Frank crossed over the bridge.

Dalton: What are you doing here?

Frank: Why, I crossed over your bridge, your very beautiful bridge. I congratulate you on your cleverness and wisdom.

Dalton: You do?

Frank: Since you were the first to bridge the gap in our communications, I thought I should be the first to step over that bridge. *(He hands Dalton the rose.)* Here, this beautiful rose is for you.

Dalton: *(touched by the gift of the rose)* You know, I've always admired your lovely garden, especially early in the morning before my noisy kids come out.

Frank: Your kids aren't so noisy.

Narrator: Frank invited Dalton over for coffee, explaining how lonely he had been since his wife died and admitting he'd been just a little jealous of Dalton with all his family. Meanwhile the forgotten carpenter was gathering his tools once again when Leroy approached.

Leroy: Excuse me, Sir, but could you stay and build my dog a dog house? Please?

Carpenter: I'm sorry, Son, I can't, though I'd love to. You see, I have other bridges to build.

BUILDING A CHURCH

What a Church Should Be

SCRIPTURE: Proverbs 3:17, Matthew 25:34-36, James 2:14-18, 1 John 3:17-18. (Selected scripture is best read immediately after the skit.)

THEME: A church is not a building, but people doing the will of God, which is to love and care for one another.

PRESENTERS: Three to five miming clowns, depending on whether the clowns play more than one role; one short speaking role and one optional scripture reader.

COSTUMES: Speakers may be in normal dress.

PROPS: Children's blocks or tinker toys or other building material such as pieces of wood or bricks; hammer, screw driver, and/or other tools; two signs, one saying "CHURCH UNDER CONSTRUCTION," the other asking for money for homeless, should be mounted so that the signs can be carried.

DIRECTOR'S NOTE: *This is a mimed clown skit.*

PRESENTATION

Clown 1 is building with blocks, completely absorbed. Nearby is a sign that states "CHURCH UNDER CONSTRUCTION."

Clown 2 enters carrying a sign asking for help for the homeless or hungry. **Clown 2** taps **Clown 1** on the shoulder.

Clown 1 scarcely looks at the sign but shakes head and returns to work on the building again.

Clowns 3 and 4, a poor mother and crying child who is injured approach **Clown 1. Clown 1** reacts to the crying child by putting hands over ears and irritably orders the two away. Shakes head at these constant intrusions and goes back to building.

Clown 5 is bullying a smaller **Clown 6. Clown 5** shoves **Clown 6,** shakes finger at **Clown 6,** pushes him or her down, and in general bullies **Clown 6. Clown 6** either rushes to **Clown 1** and pulls on sleeve for help or **Clown 6** might push **Clown 5** so that he or she falls into **Clown 1.**

Clown 1 looks up, literally brushes self off from this encounter, shakes a finger at them and mimes giving them a lecture, perhaps pointed at the church he or she is building. **Clown 5** continues to bully **Clown 6** until they are out of sight. Meanwhile, **Clown 1** returns to work.

*(Enter **Passerby**, either a clown or ordinary person who watches Clown 1 a bit and speaks):*

Passerby: What are you doing?

Clown 1:   *mimes building a church.*

Passerby: You're building a church.

*(**Clown 1** mimes love of God.)*

Passerby: You're building a church to show you love God. *(**Passerby** admires the block-building.)* That's wonderful. Keep up the good work.

As **Passerby** leaves and **Clown 1** resumes work, appropriate scripture might be read before **Clown 1** exits. James 2:14-18 is recommended.

NOTE: Purchaser may use this activity as desired as part of any service or program. Necessary photocopies of scripts and movements may be made for each presenter. There is no additional cost or fee for use by original purchaser, including the church or not-for-profit organization for which it was purchased. Use of a video or sketches for fund raising, television, radio, video, or commercial purposes is prohibited.
Copyright © 1999 Abingdon Press

SOWING SEEDS

The Parable and Its Explanation

SCRIPTURE: Matthew 13:1-23; Mark 4:3-8 and/or 4:14-20; Luke 8:4-15.

THEME: God requires that we not only listen to God's word but act upon it.

PRESENTERS: Scripture reader and four to six clowns, depending on whether two clowns play two roles each.

CHARACTERS FOR PARABLE, PART I:
Farmer, who may also be the Sun Clown
Bird Clown, who may also be Rescue Clown
Three Thorn Clowns (May be reduced to two)
Good Seed Clown

CHARACTERS FOR EXPLANATION, PART II:
Preacher Clown
Oblivious Clown (may also be Helpful Clown)
Beautiful Clown
Luxury-Loving Clown
Distracted Clown
Helpful Clown

PROPS FOR PART I, THE PARABLE: Beak and/or feather for the Bird Clown; some kind of container for the farmer's seeds; seeds; two to three forks; flashlight; stretcher, wheelchair, body bag, or just a sign that the Rescue Clown wears saying "Paramedic" or "Rescue" or "Morgue." Flower pot with nothing in it. Flower pot with plant in bloom or flower arrangement.

PROPS FOR PART II, THE EXPLANATION: Bibles for each clown; flashy jewels and beautiful fabric, whatever necessary to costume the "beautiful" clown.

DIRECTOR'S NOTE: *There are several options for this clown skit.*

1. *Both the parable and Jesus' explanation of the parable may be acted out by the same clowns or different clowns for each skit.*
2. *The first parable may be acted out as read, followed by a simple reading of Jesus' explanation.*
3. *The first parable may be read and the explanation is acted out.*
4. *The parable may be mimed only and not read, followed by Jesus' explanation.*

PRESENTATION

Note: *Clowns mime as scripture is read.*

PART I: THE PARABLE

A **Farmer** walks into the sanctuary tossing gigantic seeds as the parable is read. Already in place are a group of two or three clowns and one sitting on his or her knees with circled arms and smiling. The farmer tosses four seeds, making sure one lands within the Thorn Clowns' reach and one lands within the encircled arms of the clown representing fertile soil. The other two are thrown randomly.

After **Farmer** leaves, a **Bird Clown** dashes in, snatches up a seed, looks around to see if he/ or she is being watched, and hustles away (verse 4).

A **Sun Clown** with a flashlight enters and shines it with a fierce expression and much intensity on another seed, holding the flashlight very high, then lowering to within an inch of the seed The "dead" seed may then be picked up and held like a dead fish and/or retrieved by a **Rescue Clown** and placed on a stretcher or the equivalent, or otherwise carried out as if mortally wounded. A sign indicating the Rescue Clown is from the morgue or that he or she is an undertaker can work also (verses 5, 6).

A group of two or three clowns, the **Thorn Clowns**, surround another seed. They jab at it with forks and cover it with the forks and depart (verse 7).

The **Good Seed Clown** reveals the seed he or she has encircled all this time. The clown carries the seed like a baby, tenderly places it into a pot, may mime putting in dirt, watering, holding up to the sun, and otherwise nurturing. The clown may even rock the pot like a baby. He or she might occasionally gesture to the congregation that all is coming along nicely. Preferably unseen, the clown exchanges an empty pot for one with plant or flowers and produces "the fertile seed" for everyone to view (verse 8).

PART II: THE EXPLANATION

(Optional) Reader reads Mark 4:10-20 which may or may not be acted out.

Preacher Clown enters with a Bible, points to it and mimes preaching, stumbles and falls. He or she cannot get up (verse 14).

Enter Bible-carrying **Oblivious Clown**, reading intently. The clown notes the fallen clown and starts to go to his aid, but doesn't get there before a clown of the opposite sex comes by and flirts outrageously tipping hat, batting lashes, offering flowers. The clown either turns abruptly from the fallen clown or steps right past or right over the clown to follow the **Beautiful Clown** (verse 15).

Enter Bible-carrying **Distracted Clown** reading and grinning with joy. The clown starts toward the hurt clown but stumbles and hurts an ankle or foot. Jumping around to reveal his or her pain, the clown angrily throws the Bible down, turns and limps away (verses 16, 17).

Bible-carrying **Luxury-Loving Clown** enters, ponders, reads some more, nods affirmatively to what he's read. The clown notices the hurt person and reaches down to help him or her up and may actually have the other clown almost on his or her feet. Along comes a clown carrying sparkling jewels, beautiful fabrics, and so forth. The Clown with the Bible still in hand, turns away from the fallen clown, perhaps reluctantly, and follows the clown with luxuries. **Luxury-Loving Clown** takes a crown of jewels or a necklace and lays the Bible down to try it on, forgets the Bible, and goes off (verses 18, 19).

Enter **Helpful Clown** carrying a Bible. He or she is joyful as he or she reads but stops to ponder a word before reading again. **Helpful Clown** comes to **Preacher Clown** and helps him or her out (verse 20).

TREASURES

Interpretation of Scripture

SCRIPTURE: Matthew 6:19-21
THEME: Value people and God over things.
PRESENTERS: One teacher with memorized speaking role;
   four clowns, Clowns 1 and 4 with memorized lines.
PROPS: Props should be decided upon and collected before
   the first rehearsal. Possibilities include a jewelry box or
   treasure chest; bright, showy costume jewelry; imitation
   fur wrap; money/wallet/credit cards; poster made to look
   like a dollar bill in such a way that a tenth of it can be
   stripped away; electronic equipment such as computer
   games or video cassettes or a boom box; sports equipment such as tennis racquet, football, baseball, exercise
   equipment.

PRESENTATION

Clowns enter and busy themselves reading the Bible or
playing a game.

Enter **Teacher**, who claps hands to get their attention.

Teacher: Today we are going to talk about treasures.

Clown 1 hustles out.

Teacher: Now, where's she (he) going?

Clown 1 returns with a treasure chest and a proud grin.

Teacher: No, not that kind of treasure.

Clown 1 looks perplexed but sets chest down and sits
down.

**Teacher: Let's talk about what you treasure most in
your life. What would cause you pain or
unhappiness if you didn't have it. What do
you ask for; what do you pray for?**

All Clowns rush away to collect gifts that have been stored where they can't be seen.

Teacher: **Wait!** *(Tries to stop different clowns as they rush in and out, but finally gives up and sits down.)* **Oh, well.**

Clown 1 rushes out and returns with various items of wearing apparel such as clothing, shoes, boots, hats, jewelry.

Clown 2 rushes out and brings back books, television, computer game, videos.

Clown 3 rushes out and returns with sports equipment.

Clown 4: While all the above is going on, Clown 4 is selecting people from the congregation who have been forewarned. He or she brings each up to the front, delivers a handshake, a hug, a kiss, a pat on the head, and so forth. All these people stand clumped together, unmoving, arms around each other. After six people are collected, **Clown 1** notices and stops, walks around the group of people, peering into their faces, acting like he doesn't know what they are.

Clown 1: (to Clown 4) **What are you doing?**

Clown 4: **I'm collecting treasures.**

Clown 1: **These aren't treasures. These are people.** *(Goes to teacher, shakes head sadly.)* **He (she) needs help.** *(Goes back to clown 4, looking on sadly.)* **Look, at all our treasures. You don't have anything at all.**

Clown 4: *(stubbornly)* **I have my treasures.**

Clown 1: **I told you, these aren't treasures. THESE ARE PEOPLE.**

Clown 4: *(goes to Teacher)* **Didn't you say what we**

treasure most in life, what would cause us to be unhappy if we didn't have it, what we wished for and prayed for?

Teacher: **That's what I said.**

Clown 4: **Well, that's what I have.** *(Goes to an individual and brings him or her from the circle with each statement.)* **I prayed for courage and he (she) believed in me** *(person 1)*. **I prayed for comfort, and he (she) consoled me** *(person 2)*. **I prayed to be accepted and he (she) approved of me** *(person 3)*. **I prayed to be heard, and he (she) listened** *(person 4)*. **I asked for just a little joy, and he (she) made me laugh** *(person 5)*. **I needed love, and he (she) cared** *(person 6)*.

Teacher: **Courage, comfort, acceptance, attention, laughter, love. Yes, these are what makes the kingdom of heaven.**

Clown 2: *(with great revelation)* **Oh!** *(joins the little group of people Clown 4 has brought together, hugging and shaking hands, and so forth).*

Clown 3: *(considers momentarily and joins the group, too.)*

Clown 1: *(looks at group, at Narrator, and his or her "treasures," looking puzzled)* **I don't get it.** *(Collects some or all of the treasures and departs.)*

Optional reading of Matthew 6:19-21 by Teacher or someone else.

THE WIDOW'S MITE

Interpretation of Scripture

SCRIPTURE: Mark 12:37*b*-44 (NRSV)
THEME: Giving from the heart, not for show, is what pleases God.
PRESENTERS: One scripture reader, five miming clowns
DIRECTOR'S NOTE: *A mimed clown skit with narration.*

PRESENTATION

Narrator: **And the large crowd was listening to [Jesus] with delight. As he taught, he said, "Beware of the scribes, who like to walk around in long robes."**

Clown 1 struts in. He or she swishes a garish robe around dramatically, primping and showing off.

Narrator: **And to be greeted with respect in the marketplaces,**

Enter **Clown 5** (poor widow) and **Clown 2** from different directions so that they walk toward each other or intersect. **Clown 2** is nodding scornfully at everyone, and when he or she meets **Clown 5** either roughly motions that Clown 5 should bow before him or her or actually pushes Clown 5 into a bow.

Clown 5 rises and slowly makes her way toward the offering plate as the other clowns enter and do their thing.

Narrator: **And to have the best seats in the synagogues**

Enter **Clown 3**, who marches in and sits down up front, literally shoving someone aside, preferably the pastor.

Narrator: **And places of honor at banquets!**

Enter **Clown 4**, with a huge napkin around the neck to sit at a chair in the front of the sanctuary with knife and fork ready.

Narrator: They devour widows' houses

Clown 5 should be near **Clown 2** at this point so that **Clown 2** can shove a ledger in front of her nose or point to palm in a gesture demanding money. **Clown 5** gestures that she doesn't have it, and **Clown 2** snatches her shawl right off her shoulders.

Narrator: And for the sake of appearance say long prayers.

Clowns pray: **Clown 1** peeks to see if people are watching. **Clown 2** points to self. **Clown 3** does the thumb-in-suspender routine. **Clown 5** is in genuine prayer.

Narrator: They will receive the greater condemnation.

All but **Clown 5** look sharply at the reader, surprised and irritated.

Narrator: He sat down opposite the treasury and watched the crowd putting money into the treasury.

All clowns walk up to the plate on the altar and deposit their offering. **Clown 1** may put in a very small piece of jewelry. **Clown 2** will put in a credit card. **Clown 3** will have a huge dollar bill that he will tear a corner off of and place in the plate, and **Clown 4** will drop in some coins with a flourish. Each clown will make sure everyone sees what is being deposited in the plate.

Narrator: A poor widow came and put in two small copper coins, which are worth a penny.

Clown 5, head down, looking sad that she can't do better, puts two pennies in the plate. She kneels and prays, remaining in this position for the last verse.

Narrator: **Then he called his disciples and said to them, "Truly I tell you, this poor widow has put in more than all those who are contributing to the treasury. For all of them have contributed out of their abundance; but she out of her poverty has put in everything she had, all she had to live on."**

All clowns depart as this is read, **Clown 5** being the last to leave.

Chapter Five

SEASONAL SERVICES AND DRAMA SERIES

Let your light shine before men, that they may see your good deeds and praise your Father in heaven.

Matthew 5:16

There is little new to add to the instructions already presented for incorporating worship arts into special services such as Easter or Christmas Eve, except that people who are unfamiliar with the program tend to be more receptive to drama or dance during these times. They do not feel as threatened, believing the presentation is included to celebrate a special occasion. However, after they have experienced the arts in worship, they are usually eager to see them included in Sunday morning worship.

WEEKLY DIALOGUE FOR ADVENT INCLUDING MUSIC, DANCE, AND A COMPLETE CHRISTMAS EVE SERVICE

SCRIPTURE:
Advent 1—Luke 1:5-38: Zechariah and Mary and the Angels Who Visited Them
Theme: Acceptance

Advent 2—Matthew 1:18-25: Joseph and the Angel in His Dreams.
Theme: Risking/Hearing the Call
Advent 3—Luke 1:39-56: Mary and Elizabeth Sharing and Affirming the Call
Theme: Sharing
Advent 4—Luke 2:8-14: Angels Bring the Joyful News to the Shepherds and All People
Theme: Feeling Joy
Christmas Eve—Luke 2:1-20, Isaiah 11:1-10

THEME: The ongoing, weekly drama consists of a discussion between a narrator and a person skeptical of the truth of the Christmas story or its benefit to mankind. The fourth Advent service and Christmas Eve include a child as well.

Each Sunday, the narrator attempts to introduce or amplify the week's Advent scripture and theme but is continually interrupted and questioned by a Skeptic who can be male or female, youth or adult.

OPTIONAL CANDLE-LIGHTING THEMES: Themes coordinate with the dialogue themes each week.
Advent 1 Candle Lighting: ACCEPTING
Accepting the irrational and unbelievable on faith, without fear of what's going to be the outcome.
Advent 2 Candle Lighting: RISKING
Taking risks and taking action on faith, without the fear of criticism.
Advent 3 Candle Lighting: SHARING
Sharing the excitement, confirming the call from God, without the fear of ridicule.
Advent 4 Candle Lighting: FEELING JOY.
Feeling the joy of faith, without fear of disappointment.
Christmas Eve Candle Lighting
Review of all Advent themes.

PRESENTERS: Minimum of four: one or more scripture readers, depending on whether the scripture is told as a story or read as dialogue, and whether different people deliver the scripture each Advent Sunday. Three dramatists—two youth or adults for Advent 1, 2, 3, and

Christmas Eve and one child for the fourth Sunday in Advent and Christmas Eve. Optional dancers: one female as Mary, one male or female as the angel for first Sunday in Advent.

PROPS: Props for Advent 4 and/or Christmas Eve—a doll and blanket, a manger and stool and any other props desired for a stable scene.

MUSIC: Advent 1 includes an optional movement. Advent 4 includes ten hymn suggestions. Advent 4 can stand alone.

DIRECTOR NOTES: *Narrator and Skeptic may sit on stools or chairs if they are at a level high enough to be seen. Each week's dialogue precedes, includes, or follows the stated scripture, either read dramatically or told as story. The dialogues can be memorized or read dramatically, presented each week by the same two people or by different people. Because the Skeptic introduces doubts and questions some people fear voicing aloud, the dialogue may appear challenging or slightly radical at times; therefore, it may be a good idea to have a discussion involving the pastor, director, and presenters regarding the issues presented in the skit.*

At Church of the Saviour, the skit was presented by the same two women each worship service in Advent. They memorized the dialogue and presented the drama after only one rehearsal each week. Several weeks before Advent 1, they received the script for the first and longest dialogue. The other scripts they received after worship on the previous Sunday and rehearsed together once before the presentation the following Sunday. The narrator carried a folder with notes, which she read when the script called for it and referred to when necessary.

There is considerably more dialogue and movement in the Advent 4 presentation. This service includes ten songs interspersed throughout, which give the speakers adequate opportunity to look at their notes for the next segment of dialogue. The Skeptic did not carry any notes, even in this presentation, but a presenter playing this role might feel more comfortable keeping a folder containing a script on his or her lap or writing cue lines on index cards and tucking the cards into a Bible.

The Narrator should be self-assured and respond compassionately, though occasionally a little vexed by the interruptions of the Skeptic. The Skeptic, on the other hand, should appear childlike in her worries, not hostile, making it clear she or he wants to believe and wishes to be convinced.

The child who plays the part in Advent 4 and Christmas Eve should be energetic and bubbly. It is extremely important that he or she speak loudly, clearly, and slowly when facing the congregation for those lines that are really spoken to everybody, not just the skeptic.

It is very effective to deliver scripture during Advent as story. If your church chooses to present the following scripture lessons as story, you will need a storyteller who must know his/her scripture assignment several weeks in advance in order to memorize it.

ADVENT 1

SCRIPTURE: Luke 1:5-38: Zechariah and Mary and the Angels

Narrator: Today is the beginning of the most beautiful season of our faith—Advent or, as some people prefer to call it—Christmas. We will begin our story this year in Luke 1:5 through 38 with…

Skeptic: The fairy tale we love so much.

Narrator: Fairy tale?

Skeptic: Don't fall off your stool with shock, but I don't believe it happened.

Narrator: You don't believe what happened?

Skeptic: *(looking around to see if anyone will stone him)* You know *(lowers voice)* angels, virgin births—all that stuff.

Narrator: *(to Skeptic)* I'm sorry. This must be a dreadful time of year for you. *(to audience)* As I said earlier, we are beginning the story this year with Zechariah, husband of Elizabeth and the father of John the Baptist. An angel visited

Zechariah in much the same way the angel Gabriel visited Mary, and it is interesting to compare their reactions to these visits.

Skeptic: I don't believe in angels. They just make a pretty story, like Cinderella's godmother.

Narrator: Did you know angels are mentioned nearly three hundred times in the Bible? Did you know there are angels in Buddhist and Taoist religions, and that Gabriel is reported to have appeared to Muhammad.

Skeptic: No kidding. I thought Gabriel was ours—you know, Christians'.

Narrator: He was mentioned first in the Old Testament, by Daniel, a Jew.

Skeptic: The guy gets around.

Narrator: May I go on? *(Skeptic nods)* Zechariah pretty much demanded proof that what the angel told him was so, while Mary asked for an explanation, not doubting the angel but wanting to know how what was predicted would come to pass.

Skeptic: Yeah, she just stands there. I'm sure if I saw an angel fluttering down from heaven before my eyes, I would be out of there in a hurry. We're talking now!

Narrator: Angels aren't always winged creatures with flowing gowns. They can take other forms, including that of human beings.

Skeptic: If I were all alone, minding my own business, when suddenly a stranger appeared out of nowhere, I would run for my life. I wouldn't just stand there and listen to a little speech.

Narrator: Mary did.

Skeptic: I know she did, and that's why I don't believe the story. Her response was not realistic. She'd be scared to death.

Narrator: She was scared. So was Zechariah for that matter. The angel allayed their fear, at least enough for them to hear the message. *(to audience)* And so it was that a young virgin from...

Skeptic: Don't believe it.

Narrator: What now?

Skeptic: God doesn't defy the laws of nature—God's own laws. There's only one way for a woman to conceive a child.

Narrator: You poor thing. Don't you believe in miracles, either?

Skeptic: Absolutely not.

Narrator: *(pause, considering Skeptic curiously)* You know, people see what they're looking for.

Skeptic: You mean, if I look for miracles, I'll see them.

Narrator: Try it.

Skeptic: *(repeating sarcastically, sort of)* Try it. Listen, I don't think...

Narrator: It's time for our story, as told in the Gospel of Luke.

Skeptic: And not told in the Gospels of Mark and John. The birth of Jesus is not even mentioned in Mark and John.

Narrator: So?

Skeptic: Don't you think if it happened the way Luke says it happened, Mark and John would mention it?

Narrator: No, I don't. The Gospel writers were no different from modern biographers. Each had a specific interest in the life of Jesus and wrote about things pertaining to that interest. Let me give you a more current example. Recently I read a biography of Martin Luther King, Jr., that didn't mention a thing about his birth except the date. The writer focused on the events of King's ministry. To learn about the circumstances of King's birth, you would have to read another account of his life. You understand what I'm saying?

Skeptic: Well, of course I do, but I think you are simplifying the issue.

Narrator: And I think it's time for our story.

Luke 1:5-38 is read as dialogue scripture or told by a storyteller.

(For optional Mary/Angel Dance, see chapter 3, page 96.)

ADVENT 2

SCRIPTURE: Matthew 1:18-25: Joseph and the Angel in His Dreams.

NOTE: *It is best if the scripture is read immediately before the Narrator and Skeptic present their dialogue.*

Narrator: The people living at the time of the birth of Jesus overcame fear time and again to act in response to what God called them to do.

Skeptic: Like they had a choice.

Narrator: The people then, as now, enjoyed free will.

Skeptic: You're telling me Mary and Joseph could have

said, "No thanks" and God would have said, "Oh, sorry. I'll ask someone else." Come on.

Narrator: I don't know the answer to that because they didn't say no thanks. I do know that people of the Bible have responded to God's calls in a number of less courageous ways. Jonah, for instance, ran away and tried to hide. Moses argued and fussed. Samuel had to be called three times before he even heard the message. Zechariah scoffed at the message. God's calls always involve risk, and people are often afraid. Both Mary and Joseph were afraid, but they overcame their fear to accept the message.

Skeptic: I don't see what Joseph had to fear.

Narrator: Oh, really? It wouldn't trouble you to defy convention because of a message you heard from God.

Skeptic: I don't get any messages from God.

Narrator: No? Have you never been called to accept a change in your life you didn't understand or to take a role that you didn't ask for or especially want?

Skeptic: Well, sure, but...

Narrator: And were you afraid?

Skeptic: *(hesitant to admit)* Maybe.

Narrator: And did you go ahead, even though you were afraid, doing what you felt God called you to do?

Skeptic: Now, wait a minute. Who said anything about God. The things I'm talking about are not commands from God. I'm talking about...

Narrator: Something that came to you in a dream, maybe? Or in a reflective moment in the sanctuary, or . . .

Skeptic: We're talking about Joseph. He wasn't being asked to do something especially risky.

Narrator: He was being asked to overcome his initial shock and sense of betrayal. He was being called to believe and to accept parenting a special child. He couldn't have understood what it might mean for Jesus to one day save people from their sins, but he didn't insist on understanding. He obeyed God and did what he was told to do.

Skeptic: And this Christmas story is telling me that's what I'm supposed to do. Is that the message?

Narrator: I don't do messages. Angels do messages. And pastors. Let's listen and see what we're being called to do.

Pastor Message

ADVENT 3

SCRIPTURE: Luke 1:39-56: Mary And Elizabeth Sharing and Affirming the Call.

Narrator: Today, this third Sunday in Advent, we will be talking about friendship and sharing.

Skeptic: I thought this was Elizabeth Sunday.

Narrator: There is no such thing as Elizabeth Sunday.

Skeptic: Well, there ought to be. This is one part of the Christmas story that makes sense to me. A very young woman is pregnant with her first child and rushes to talk about it to another woman.

Narrator: Elizabeth lived in Judea, some four days traveling distance from Mary. Why wouldn't she have rushed to her mother or a sister or a good friend in Nazareth?

Skeptic: At times like these, a person needs to talk to someone else, preferably someone in the same or similar circumstances.

Narrator: Very good. Want to hear the story?

Skeptic: Why do you ask? I'm going to hear it whether I want to or not.

Narrator: (pats Skeptic's head or gives Skeptic a look of indulgence. Narrator and Skeptic may remain in place during the following.)

Luke 1:39-56 may be read or told as story. A song such as "Tell Out My Soul" may be included here before, after, or in place of the Magnificat.

Narrator: Beautiful, wasn't it?

Skeptic: Sure, but why didn't Mary sing out her joy when she first heard she was going to bear a savior?

Narrator: I think she needed time to take it all in.

Skeptic: I think she didn't really believe it until Elizabeth confirmed it for her.

Narrator: And I think God means for us to seek each other for support. Ever notice that the Bible doesn't speak of people living in isolation, going it alone. But rather, they interacted. They needed each other, and through each other they found God. That's why Elizabeth was so important. She let Mary express who she was and what she felt openly.

Skeptic: And what about poor old Zechariah? Is he still without speech?

Narrator: Yes.

Skeptic: Figures. The women are talking and singing while the man sits in silence.

Narrator: It was his own fault, you know, doubting God. But don't worry about it. When Elizabeth's son was born, Zechariah went against custom to name the baby John as instructed by an angel. At that point, he received the gift of speech once more and sang his own song. That make you happy?

Skeptic: Yes, as a matter of fact. I don't believe in loose ends.

Narrator: Or miracles or angels. For Christmas you want neat transparent packages, solid and defined.

Skeptic: Wrapped in see-through paper.

Narrator: Nothing unexplained.

Skeptic: No surprises.

Narrator: No joy.

ADVENT 4

SCRIPTURE: Luke 2:8-14: Angles Bring the Joyful News to the Shepherds and All People

PRESENTERS: The characters include, in addition to Narrator and Skeptic, a child, male or female.

PROPS: A doll with blanket. If dialogue is to conclude on Christmas Eve rather than today, a manger and stool or bale of hay are necessary with any other stable decorations that are wanted.

This skit can be presented as part of a Cantata, or several or all of the hymns may be deleted. Music may be sung by a choir, soloists, or the congregation. Hymns are suggested below, however, and alternative hymns or contemporary songs with similar themes can easily be substituted.

The dialogue has two optional endings: (1) If the Skeptic and Narrator will be participants in a Christmas Eve service, there is an ending leading into Christmas Eve, involving a manger scene that can be extremely simple, consisting of little more than a manger. (2) The other ending concludes the dialogue on the fourth Sunday in Advent and does not involve props other than a doll.

Narrator and Skeptic *take their places on two stools in front. There is another stool nearby for the* **Child**.

Narrator: Today, the fourth Sunday in Advent, is a special celebration. We anticipate the birth of the Christ Child with great excitement and joy.

Skeptic: Maybe you do, but I don't. And I'll bet there are a whole lot of people out there who don't either. Some people would just like this whole thing to be over with.

Narrator: There seems to be something lacking in your Christmas spirit.

Skeptic: And don't start delivering the Scrooge lecture. I'm not anticipating anything but huge bills on my credit cards and squabbles among my relatives at Christmas dinner. I don't feel joyful. I don't feel much of anything.

Narrator: *(thinks a second before speaking)* Do me a favor. Set all that aside for right now. Don't think about dinners and credit cards and relatives.

	Just listen to the music. Can you do that? Just listen and look at what's around you?
Skeptic:	I guess.
Narrator:	Good. Then let song fill the air.
Song 1:	"There's a Song in the Air"
Narrator:	Do you feel it? The Joy? The celebration?
Skeptic:	I want to. I really do. Everyone is so happy, but...
Narrator:	You're afraid.
Skeptic:	Of course not. Why would I be afraid? *(pause)* All right. Yes, I think I am afraid.
Narrator:	Of what?
Skeptic:	The joy? The joy. If I know the joy, my life will have to change. Won't it?
Narrator:	Yes.
Skeptic:	I don't know. Who is this baby, really? Who is he?
Narrator:	He's called many things: a counselor, a prince of peace, a king, a savior *(pause)*. What kind of child is this to you?
Song 2:	"What Child Is This"
Skeptic:	I don't know how I can believe that this baby is born to be a king or a savior, not for me, personally, anyway.
Narrator:	Maybe you have to believe in miracles first.
Skeptic:	I know: To see a miracle, I must be looking for one.
Narrator:	Look from the heart, not the head. Be like Mary and just accept what's given.
Song 3:	"To a Maid Engaged to Joseph"

Skeptic: So beautiful, the whole idea of it, so beautiful!

Narrator: Yes, it is. Do you want more?

Skeptic: Yes.

Narrator: You're not afraid anymore?

Skeptic: Yes I am, but I'm ready to hear, to see. *(hesitantly)* I think.

Narrator: Then, make way for the angels.

Song 4: "Angels We Have Heard on High"

*Enter **Child** carrying a doll wrapped in a blanket. She carries it tenderly, lovingly, like a baby preferably; she walks to the Skeptic and hands her the doll. The **Skeptic** shies away from the doll as if it would burn her. The **Child** is persistent, thrusting the doll toward the **Skeptic**.*

Child: Go ahead, take it. *(pause while Skeptic hesitantly takes the doll, holding it very uncomfortably)* I know. It's just a doll. Everyone uses dolls at Christmastime. They represent the baby Jesus. All you have to do is see a real, live baby, instead of the doll. You see it in your mind. It's not hard. And then you remember that the baby is Jesus, and that Jesus came to show us how to love. That's all. It's not hard. Just don't think like a grown up. Think like me. *(she starts to leave)*

Skeptic: *(calls to **Child**)* Hey!

Child: You want me to stay?

Skeptic: *(holds doll out for **Child** to take. **Child** ignores the gesture and the obvious desire of the Skeptic: that she leave.)* Okay, I'll stay. **Child** returns, pulls up a stool and takes a seat but does not take the doll. **Child** looks at the choir or at someone in the congregation when **Skeptic** tries to hand it to her.)*

Skeptic: Listen, I don't want...

Child: *(finger to lips)* Shhh.

(Lights are lowered for next song, and Skeptic settles down, a little embarrassed.)

Song 5: "Away in a Manger"

Child: Now, the baby Jesus is asleep, and the shepherds go and tell all their friends what happened.

Skeptic: While they tell all their friends what happened, you want to hold this doll?

Child: Baby.

Skeptic: Just take it.

Child: Shhh. *(finger to lips, again)* They're going to sing.

Skeptic: *(turns to Narrator and whispers as congregation or choir prepare to sing)*

Song 6: "While Shepherds Watched Their Flocks"

Child: The shepherds were mostly kids, you know.

Skeptic: Will you please take this doll.

Child: Baby.

Skeptic: *(to Narrator)* You can jump in here any time.

Narrator: And do what?

Skeptic: Get rid of this kid.

Narrator: Jesus said, "Let the little children come to me, and do not hinder them."

Skeptic: Oh, please.

Narrator: Maybe God came to us through an infant because he loved children so much.

Song 7: "Good Christian Friends, Rejoice"

Skeptic: There it is, that joy, again. All these Christmas songs speak of joy and rejoicing; yet, this world is a suffering place. Don't deny it.

Narrator: It is a suffering place. The more a person suffers, the more joy he is able to feel at this gift.

Skeptic: I don't understand that.

Narrator: You don't need to understand. Think with your heart.

Child: Think like me.

Song 8: "Sing We Now of Christmas"

Child: I just love Christmas.

Skeptic: Sure you do. Who doesn't. All the lights, the presents, the parties. Time off work and school.

Child: Yeah. And all cause of Jesus.

Skeptic: No. Not (imitates **Child**) cause of Jesus. People would do all those things if they weren't celebrating the birth of Jesus. Most of them do, in fact. It would be exactly the same.

Narrator: No it wouldn't.

Skeptic: Okay, so there would be no reason to go to church on Christmas Eve. What else?

Narrator: Hope. With the birth of the Prince of Peace, we are given hope.

Skeptic: Hope. Accept. Believe. It's asking a lot.

Child: I hope for lots of things. It's easy.

Narrator: Did you know there are at least thirty specific references to hope in the Bible. Like this one:

"The God of hope fill you with all joy and peace in believing, that ye may abound in hope." And this one: "Faith is the substance of things hoped for, the evidence of things not seen."

Skeptic: Then faith comes from hope.

Narrator: Try it.

Child: Try it.

Song 9: "Love Came Down at Christmas"

*If Advent 4 is to be the last dialogue presentation, **Skeptic** and **Child** might walk out together, **Skeptic** holding doll more like a baby, or the **Child** could show him or her how to carry it. The **Narrator** may exit however director wishes.*

● *If **Narrator**, **Skeptic**, and **Child** are to be a part of the Christmas Eve service, dialogue continues:*

Child: It's time to put up the manger scene. You want to help?

Skeptic: I don't think so.

Child: Okay. You want to hold the baby, then? We don't put him in the manger until Christmas Eve. (***Child** scampers off. Child may or may not assist as a manger scene is set up in a place in the sanctuary where it can remain until Christmas Eve. The scene can be very simple, consisting of a stool or other object for sitting and an empty manger. Oil lamps, candles, blankets, straw, or anything else depicting a stable can be added. All or most items could already be in place but covered so that putting the manger scene together requires only uncovering the items. All of this may occur during the dialogue or at any point thereafter.)*

Skeptic: *(to Narrator:)* She will come back to get this doll, right?

Narrator: Baby. In that child's eyes, you are holding the baby Jesus. Can you, just for a moment, see through that child's eyes?

Skeptic: *(holds the doll up and studies it, then speaks, sounding very disappointed)* I just see a doll.

Child: I'll take the baby now. *(**Child** is given the doll)* I get to put him in the manger on Christmas Eve. It's a very special privilege. *(privilege is enunciated very carefully)* That's what my mom says. *(**Child** turns to go, stops and comes back, speaks hesitantly.)* Maybe...if you come to church Christmas Eve, I'll let you put the baby in the manger. If you want. *(pause)* Maybe. *(**Child** skips out.)*

Song 10: "Hark! the Herald Angels Sing"

Benediction

CHRISTMAS EVE

Suggested Call to Worship: Isaiah 11:1-10
> Scripture read with congregation chorusing something like: "Jesus is the Spirit" after verses 1-3, "Jesus is righteousness" after verses 4-5, "Jesus is peace" after verses 6-10.

Silent Time with Music:
Child emerges with the doll that represents Jesus and walks with it to the waiting manger. The **Child** carefully arranges the blanket around the doll and places it tenderly in the manger. She remains in prayerful position, maybe rearranging blanket while Advent candles are lit.

One person lights a candle, another standing back reads what the candle stands for: examples, based on previous narrator-skeptic dialogues and themes:
1. We accept the news. God has sent us his son.

2. We hear God's message and risk-taking action in the name of this child, Jesus.

3. We share this birth with others because it is our sacred responsibility.

4. We become children, expressing our joy.

Hymn, "O Come, All Ye Faithful"

Narrator: And now, it's time for the Christmas story.

(She or he reads Luke 2:1-7. When finished, she pauses and stares at Skeptic, waiting for an argument. **Skeptic** *is staring at the manger scene.)*

Narrator: No comment? No argument?

*(***Skeptic*** says nothing, doesn't appear to even have heard.* ***Child****, ministering to the "baby" looks up and locks eyes with* ***Skeptic****. She picks up the doll and takes it to the Skeptic.)*

Child: *(handing the doll to Skeptic)* I forgot. I said you could put Jesus in the manger if you want to. *(***Skeptic*** takes doll.).* Go ahead. *(Skeptic: doesn't move.)* You want me to go with you? *(***Skeptic*** looks at Narrator.)*

Narrator: How is it going to hurt you to put that baby in the manger?

Child: Come on. I'll take you.

*(***Skeptic*** takes* ***Child's*** *hand and the two approach manger. They kneel and* ***Skeptic*** *places doll in the manger.)*

Child: You're lucky. Some people never get to lay the baby Jesus in the manger their whole lives.

Skeptic: Some people never find a child to lead them.

Hymn: "Joy to the World"

Skeptic: Joy. How can we feel joy with the miserable state the world is in? Violence and persecution go on, the sickness and grief. How can we honestly feel joy in this reality?

Narrator: We don't feel joy IN reality. We feel joy despite reality. Listen.

Reading of a poem, psalm, or scripture or singing of a song that refers to joy in knowing Christ.

Skeptic: It's a beautiful night, the sanctuary is so pretty, the music, everything, I don't want to ruin things for these people, but, I have a question, and . . .

Narrator: You're worried your questions might shatter someone's faith?

Skeptic: Well, yes.

Narrator: Faith isn't weakened by questions; it's made stronger.

Skeptic: All right then, if Joseph came from Bethlehem, wouldn't his family have offered a room to one of their own?

Narrator: Let me ask you a question, first. If you were required to return to the home of your ancestors to register to vote, where would you stay?

Skeptic: In a motel. All my ancestors are dead.

Narrator: They didn't have a whole lot of motels in Bethlehem.

Skeptic: But a stable? A manger?

Narrator: Let me read you something.

Narrator: *(reads)* Bethlehem was overcrowded. Joseph and Mary probably traveled very slowly due to her condition, getting into the city very late after every available sleeping space was taken. Caves outside the city were used as holding places for livestock, and it was not uncommon for shepherds to seek shelter in one of them in inclemate weather. It makes sense that others might consider using caves for shelter an acceptable idea as well. The rich, traveling in caravans, often stopped for the night at the only inn in Bethlehem and might very well have sent servants ahead to reserve space. But Joseph and Mary were not among the rich. With no place else to go, they would have been satisfied to stay in a clean stable or cave.[1]

Narrator: So you see, for the people in those days, such an event as described here in Luke, wasn't all that unusual.

Skeptic: *(staring at the manger scene again)* I guess the writer is trying to tell me . . . us . . . that this child was one of the common folks.

Narrator: Yes, you might say, just like us.

Hymn: "Infant Holy, Infant Lowly"

Narrator: Jesus has been born. He sleeps in a cave-stable watched over by his parents. It's a beautiful picture if you let yourself see.

Hymn: "Rock-a-Bye, My Dear Little Boy"

Luke 2:8-14 Dramatically read or told as story

Hymn: "Hark! the Herald Angels Sing"

Luke 2:15-20 Dramatically read or told as story

Hymn: "The First Noel"

Skeptic: Angels again.

Narrator: Yes, angels.

Skeptic: Why is it so hard to believe? A little while ago, I put a baby in the manger and for a moment, I believed like a child; but now, it's me, an adult with a mind that won't let me be at peace.

Narrator: Do you remember what Jesus told the disciples once: *(**Narrator** may read this passage from Matthew 18:3)* "I tell you the truth, unless you change and become like little children, you will never enter the kingdom of heaven. Therefore, whoever humbles himself like this child is the greatest in the kingdom of heaven."

Child: *(holding out her hand)* You just need to hold on to Jesus. Then you won't feel so bad. Come on. I'll take you to the manger. *(**Skeptic** takes **Child's** hand, and they move back to manger. **The Child** picks up the doll and gives it tenderly to **Skeptic**. **Skeptic** may sit on stool or kneel at manger.)*

Prayer that addresses the hearts struggling to accept.

Lighting of the candles: Child may hold the candle others light from and/or light the candle of the **Skeptic**.

Hymn: "Silent Night, Holy Night"

Benediction

1. *Jesus and His Times* (Pleasantville, N.Y.: Reader's Digest Association, 1987), pp. 21, 22 and *Great People of the Bible and How They Lived* (Pleasantville, N.Y.: Reader's Digest Association, 1974), p. 321.

MAUNDY THURSDAY SERVICE

Drama with Movement

SCRIPTURE: Taken from John 13:1-10, 12-17, 37-38;
   Matthew 26:31-35; Luke 22:41-45
PRESENTERS: Three: Narrator for readings, Jesus (parts
   memorized), Peter (parts memorized)
VOICES: Two or more voices with two or three words spo-
   ken from the congregation
PROPS: Twelve candles, already lit, plus a Christ candle
SUGGESTED SETTING: Lights are dimmed for the service
   and lowered further as Jesus hands the lit candles to the
   disciples. Lights may be completely darkened when last
   disciples extinguish their candles.
MUSIC: Music from Taizé, "Stay Here."

*(Taizé music is available at most religious bookstores or may be ordered
from the Taizé Community, 1520 Taizé, France.)*

DRAMA

PART I: WASHING OF PETER'S FEET

Narrator will read John 13:1-5.

Jesus: Simon Peter. Come. It is your turn.

Peter: *(Peter may be sitting in a pew with the congrega-
             tion and will stand.)* Lord, are you going to
             wash my feet?

Jesus: You do not realize now what I am doing, but
             later you will understand.

Peter: No, you shall never wash my feet.

Jesus: Unless I wash you, you have no part with me.

Peter: *(moving toward Jesus reluctantly)* Then, Lord, not just
             my feet but my hands and my head as well.

Jesus: *(smiling as one does when one's child misunderstands)* A person who has had a bath needs only to wash his feet; his whole body is clean. And you are clean *(looks up at congregation)* though not every one of you.

(Jesus may now remove Peter's sandals and wash his feet, or invite the congregation to a hand washing, or move ahead to part II.)

OPTIONAL HAND WASHING RITUAL

Jesus: *(to congregation)* Come. Let your servant wash your hands to prepare you for the evening meal.

(Jesus, assisted by Peter, the narrator, and pastor wash and dry the hands of congregation, or they begin the process, followed by other members of the drama who have rehearsed, followed by the congregation who wash each other's hands. When finished Jesus speaks to congregation.)

PART II

Jesus: *(speaking at first to Peter, then to congregation as well)* Do you understand what I have done for you? You call me "Teacher" and "Lord," and rightly so, for that is what I am. Now that I, your Lord and Teacher, have washed your [hands and] feet, you also should wash one another's. I have set you an example that you should do as I have done for you. I tell you the truth, no servant is greater than his master, nor is a messenger greater than the one who sent him. Now that you know these things, you will be blessed if you do them.

(Communion, if desired, may be placed here, or proceed to Part III.)

PART III

Jesus: *(to congregation and Peter, who is sitting among them)* This very night you will all fall away on account of me.

Peter: [Not me, Lord.] Even if all fall away on account of you [or: the rest of them leave you,] I never will.

Jesus: [Peter,] this very night, before the rooster crows, you will disown me three times.

(Jesus begins to depart, stops to hear Peter out, smiles and shakes head and exits.)

Peter: No. You are wrong, Jesus. Even if I have to die with you, I will never disown you. [Never] *(follows Jesus).*

Voice 1: Nor will we, Lord.

Voice 2: Never.

Hymn: suggested hymn, "Dear Jesus, in Whose Life I See"

*(At conclusion of the hymn, enter **Jesus** followed by **Disciples**. They walk slowly around the altar or wherever appropriate. **Jesus** stops, facing the congregation. The **Disciples** circle him and kneel at the communion rail or in a semicircle in front of Jesus.*

*One by one, **Jesus** blesses the disciples by placing his palms down on their heads, two at a time. Jesus then raises the two disciples and gives each person a candle. As he does so, he recites the following lines as shown.)*

Jesus: *(giving candles 1 and 2.)* I am the light of the world. Follow me.

Jesus: *(candles 3 and 4)* I am the bread of life. Believe in me.

Jesus: *(candles 5 and 6)* I am the vine, you are the branches. Go and bear fruit.

Jesus: *(candles 7 and 8)* I am the good shepherd. Trust me.

Jesus: *(candles 9 and 10)* I am the teacher. Hear me.

Jesus: *(candles 11 and 12)* I am the servant. Go and do likewise.

(Jesus steps back and speaks to the disciples.)

Jesus: Stay and keep watch while I pray.

*(**Jesus** takes the Christ candle and moves away from the **Disciples**. He looks back once, then turns and moves further away, stopping at a point where he can be seen by the congregation and kneels to pray silently.*

*When **Jesus** first moves away, the **Disciples** gesture towards Jesus and appear to ask each other what's going on. One or two may take a step toward him when he stops and looks back, but **Jesus** raises a hand and stops them, or they may be held back by another.)*

Taizé Hymn: "Stay Here"[1]

*(May be sung or played on tape. During the song, the **Disciples** circle the altar or move randomly about with lit candles. They begin moving slower and slower until they stop altogether. While **Jesus** silently continues to pray, one by one, they blow out a candle and fall asleep, slumping to the floor in various positions.) (The following, based on scripture text from John 17:11, 13, 23 and Luke 22:42 may be read by someone out of sight, with appropriate movement and gestures by **Jesus,** or recited from memory by **Jesus**.)*

Jesus or Reader: Holy Father, protect them by the power of your name ... so that they may be one as we are one. I am coming to you now, but I say these things while I am still in the world, so that they may have the full measure of my joy within them. I in them and you in me. May they be brought to complete unity to let the world know that you sent me and

have loved them even as you have loved me
(long pause). Father, if you are willing, take this
cup from me *(pause);*
yet not my will, but yours be done.

*(**Jesus** blows out the Christ candle and all lights are doused
completely. A dim light may stay on **Jesus** kneeling. The song,
"Stay Here," may be sung or played again, or "Jesus, Remember
Me.")*

Benediction

*(If possible, lights should remain dim as people leave the sanctu-
ary. The **Disciples** and **Jesus** may remain in their positions
until all have departed.)*

1. *Laudate: Music of Taizé,* produced by Veritas Productions, 7/8 Lr Abbey
Street, Dublin, Ireland

GOOD FRIDAY SERVICE

THE LAST WORDS OF CHRIST

With Monologues by Mary, the Mother of Jesus

(Previously published as part of *I Pray I Ponder*, a series of monologues by Linda M. Goens. Colorado Springs: Contemporary
Drama, 1994.)

SCRIPTURE: Read as dialogue. In order of readings:
Matthew 26:57-67, 27:1-24, 26-35, 37; Luke 23:32-34, 36-
43; John 19:25-27; Mark 15:33-34; John 19:28; Luke
23:45-46; John 19:30

PRESENTERS: Nine to six readers, Mary, two who place symbols and snuff candles.

Reader 1: Narrator, Crowd. Narrator should excel as an expressive reader who can deliver the closing lines with the drama it deserves.

Reader 2: Judas, Crowd, Soldiers, Criminal 1 on cross.

Reader 3: Priest/Elders/Sanhedrin, Crowd, Criminal 2 on cross.

Reader 4: High Priest/Caiaphas, Governor/Pilate, Soldiers, the Soldier at the cross who mocks Jesus to save himself.

Reader 5: Jesus

Reader 6: False Witness, Pilate's wife, Crowd. (This part can be read by the narrator if desired.)

Symbol Placers should place symbols without compassion. Expressions should relate to the item, itself. For example, the bowl and towel would be placed carefully as a servant might do while the whip would be snapped first and placed harshly as a soldier might.

MARY delivers her monologues from anywhere; but once she has entered the sanctuary, she should remain during readings and action.

PROPS: Six stools (or chairs if on stage or platform), seven candles, candle snuffer. Symbols may include the following: pouch with coins, wash basin and pitcher with towel, whip, crown of thorns (grapevine sold in craft stores for making wreaths works well as a crown of thorns), scarlet robe, staff, chalice or sponge or both, nails, dice, self-standing sign reading, "INRI, King of the Jews."

COSTUMES: Readers may wear ordinary street clothes, but it is recommended they dress similarly in like colors, dark trousers with black, gray, tan, or white turtlenecks or long-sleeved jerseys. Mary should be in costume appropriate to biblical times. Symbol placers should be in all black, if possible.

SUGGESTED SETTING: Sanctuary lights should be dim. The seven candles may be arranged in any manner, individually in holders or together in a candelabrum as long as they are visible to the congregation. Readers may sit on stools to one side or anywhere that they do not block the placing of the symbols, the candle extinguishing, and

Mary's presentations. Symbols may be placed on an altar or table, centralized and visible.

MUSIC: Suggested hymns: "Go to Dark Gethsemane," verses 1-3, "Ah, Holy Jesus," "Were You There," "What Wondrous Love Is This." Hymns may be instrumental or sung by the congregation, the choir, or a soloist.

DANCE: Optional dance referenced.

THE DRAMA

Narrator: Those who had arrested Jesus took him to Caiaphas, the high priest, where the teachers of the law and the elders had assembled. But Peter followed him at a distance, right up to the courtyard of the high priest. He entered and sat down with the guards to see the outcome.

The chief priests and the whole Sanhedrin were looking for false evidence against Jesus so that they could put him to death. But they did not find any.

Finally two false witnesses came forward.

Reader 6 (False Witness): This fellow said, "I am able to destroy the temple of God and rebuild it in three days."

Narrator: The high priest stood up and said to Jesus:

Reader 4 (High Priest): Are you not going to answer? What is this testimony that these [people] are bringing against you? ...*(pause)* I charge you under oath by the living God: Tell us if you are the Christ, the Son of God.

Reader 5 (Jesus): Yes. It is as you say. But I say to all of you: In the future you will see the Son of Man sitting at the right hand of the Mighty One and coming on the clouds of heaven.

Reader 4 (High Priest): Blasphemy! Why do we need

any more witnesses? Look, now you have heard the blasphemy. What do you think?

Reader 2 (Sanhedrin): He is worthy of death.

Narrator: Then they spit in his face and struck him with their fists. Others slapped him and said:

Reader 3 (Sanhedrin): Prophesy to us, Christ. Who hit you?

Narrator: Early in the morning, all the chief priests and the elders of the people came to the decision to put Jesus to death. They bound him, led him away and handed him over to Pilate, the governor.

When Judas, who had betrayed him, saw that Jesus was condemned, he was seized with remorse and returned the thirty silver coins to the chief priests and elders.

Reader 2 (Judas): I have sinned for I have betrayed innocent blood.

Reader 3 (Priests): What is that to us? That's your responsibility.

Narrator: So Judas threw the money into the temple and left. Then he went away and hanged himself.

(Symbol 1, the pouch, tossed onto the table in such a way that the coins rattle and slide out. The more noise, the better.)

Narrator: *(continuing)* Meanwhile, Jesus stood before the governor, and the governor asked him:

Reader 4 (Governor): Are you the king of the Jews?

Jesus: Yes, it is as you say.

Narrator: When he was accused by the chief priests and the elders, he gave no answer.

Reader 4 (Governor/Pilate): Don't you hear the testimony they are bringing against you?

Narrator: But Jesus made no reply, not even to a single charge—to the great amazement of the governor. *(pause)* Now it was the governor's custom at the Feast to release a prisoner chosen by the crowd. At that time, they had a notorious prisoner, called Barabbas. So when the crowd had gathered, Pilate asked them:

Reader 4 (Pilate): Which one do you want me to release to you: Barabbas, or Jesus who is called Christ?

Narrator: For he knew it was out of envy that they had handed Jesus over to him. While Pilate was sitting on the judge's seat, his wife sent him this message:

Reader 6 (Pilate's Wife): Don't have anything to do with that innocent man, for I have suffered a great deal today in a dream because of him.

Narrator: But the chief priests and the elders persuaded the crowd to ask for Barabbas and to have Jesus executed.

Reader 4 (Pilate): Which of the two do you want me to release to you?

Readers 1, 2, 3, 6 (the crowd): Barabbas!

(Note: The Crowd should respond as a crowd, not trying to speak exactly in unison.)

Reader 4 (Pilate): What shall I do, then, with Jesus who is called Christ?

Readers 1, 2, 3, 6 (the crowd): *(more demanding)* Crucify him! *(Repeat, if desired.)*

Reader 4 (Pilate): Why? What crime has he committed?

Readers 1, 2, 3, 6 (the crowd): *(loud and vicious)* Crucify him!

Narrator: When Pilate saw that he was getting nowhere, but that instead an uproar was starting, he took water and washed his hands in front of the crowd.

Reader 4 (Pilate): I am innocent of this man's blood. It is your responsibility.

(Placement of symbol 2, wash basin and pitcher with towel, placed neatly and precisely as a servant might do for a wealthy person)

Narrator: Then he released Barabbas to them. But he had Jesus flogged and handed him over to be crucified. *(symbol 3, whip, placed firmly, perhaps with one lash in the air first)*

Narrator: *(continuing)* Then the governor's soldiers took Jesus into the Praetorium and gathered the whole company of soldiers around him. They stripped him and put a scarlet robe on him. *(symbol 4, scarlet robe, neatly draped over the table)*

Narrator: *(continuing)* and then twisted together a crown of thorns and set it on his head. *(symbol 5, crown of thorns, placed carefully near the robe, as if arranging an ensemble)*

Narrator: *(continuing)* They put a staff in his right hand and knelt in front of him and mocked him.

Readers 2, 4 (Soldiers): Hail, king of the Jews!

Narrator: They spit on him and took the staff and struck him on the head again and again. After they had mocked him, they took off the robe and put his own clothes on him. Then they led him away to crucify him. *(Symbol 6, a staff or rod of some kind. This might be smacked into the*

> *palm of one hand, a gesture indicating someone is
> about to be beaten.)*

Optional: Soldiers' Dance, chapter 3, page 100

*(**Hymn** or other appropriate musical interlude: suggested hymn,
"Go to Dark Gethsemane," verses 1-3, or "Sacred Head Now
Wounded". During the last verse, Mary enters)*

Mary: Peter! Andrew! Where were you? John! James!
How could you let this happen? But no, it isn't
your fault. It is Pilate. He is to blame. No, not
just Pilate. All of you. All of you who stood in
the courtyard are to blame. When Pilate
washed his hands of responsibility, didn't you
wash your hands of it too? Didn't you tell yourself, "I can't do anything. This is not my fault.
This is not my doing." And then you stood and
watched the whip tear apart my son's back.
The whole crowd of you just watched—and
did nothing but moan and wail. Did you think
your cries would remove my son's pain? When
the soldiers pushed that crown of thorns on his
head and the blood ran down into his eyes, did
you turn away so you wouldn't have to suffer
his humiliation, his pain? *(pause)* Did he not feel
it because you did not?

Hymn: Suggested hymns, "O Sacred Head, Now
Wounded" or "Ah, Holy Jesus"

Narrator: As they were going out, they met a man from
Cyrene, named Simon, and they forced him
to carry the cross. They came to a place
called Golgotha, which means, The Place of
the Skull. *(Symbol 7, three nails, placed in such a
way that people can see them)*

Narrator: *(continuing)* There they offered Jesus wine to
drink, mixed with gall; but after tasting it, he

refused to drink it. *(Symbol 8, large natural sponge or chalice)*

Narrator: *(continuing)* When they had crucified him, they divided up his clothes by casting lots. *(Symbol 9, a pair of dice, rolled in hands, maybe blown on for luck, and tossed)*

Narrator: *(continuing)* Above his head, they placed the written charge against him: "THIS IS JESUS, THE KING OF THE JEWS." *(Symbol 10, the sign reading INRI)*

Hymn: Suggested hymn, "Were You There"

Mary: Why didn't you fight for him? Why didn't you rescue him. I don't understand how this happened. He has committed no crime. He is an innocent man. And they are executing him. He dies for nothing, and you—all of you—remain silent. Why? You didn't even carry his cross. It was so heavy, he staggered. Did you see him stumble and fall? A stranger carried it for him. Where were you? He carried your burdens often enough. Why couldn't you carry his just this once? You are cowards. Cowards. John—you said you loved him. You said you'd do anything for him. Peter—big, brash Peter—where were you when they drove nails into my son's hands? My God, my God, I cannot bear this pain.

Narrator: Two other men, both criminals, were also led out with him to be executed . . . one on his right, the other on his left *(pause)*. Jesus said,

Reader 5: "Father, forgive them, for they do not know what they are doing." *(Candle 1 is extinguished by Symbol Placer.)*

Mary: Forgive me. Forgive us all.

Narrator: The soldiers also came up and mocked him.

Reader 4 (Soldier): If you are the king of the Jews, save yourself.

Narrator: One of the criminals who hung there hurled insults at him:

Reader 2 (Criminal 1): and us.

Narrator: But the other criminal rebuked him.

Reader 3 (Criminal 2): Don't you fear God, since you are under the same sentence? We are punished justly, for we are getting what our deeds deserve, but this man has done nothing wrong *(pause)*. Jesus, remember me when you come into your kingdom.

Reader 5 (Jesus): I tell you the truth, today you will be with me in paradise. *(Candle 2 is extinguished.)*

Mary: You calmed the storm that could have drowned all of you in the Sea of Galilee. You turned from the very edge of a cliff in Nazareth and walked right through a murderous mob. You could save yourself now, but I know you will not. I just don't know why *(freeze)*.

Narrator: Near the cross of Jesus stood his mother, his mother's sister, Mary the wife of Clopas, and Mary Magdalene. When Jesus saw his mother there, and the disciple whom he loved standing nearby, he said to his mother:

Jesus: Dear woman, here is your son *(pause)* . . . Here is your mother.

Narrator: From that time on, this disciple took her into his home. *(Candle 3 extinguished.)*

Mary: Oh, John, hold me. Take away this terrible pain.

Narrator: At the sixth hour darkness came over the whole land until the ninth hour. And at the ninth hour Jesus cried out in a loud voice:

Jesus: My God, my God! why have you forsaken me? *(Candle 4 is extinguished.)*

Mary: My God, why have you forsaken us all?

Jesus: I am thirsty. *(Candle 5 is extinguished.)*

Mary: If only I could hold fresh, cool water to your lips, my beloved son, but I can do nothing. Nothing.

Narrator: The sun stopped shining. And the curtain of the temple was torn in two. Jesus called out with a loud voice:

Jesus: Father, into your hands I commit my spirit. *(Candle 6 is extinguished.)*

Mary: Yes, my God, release him from this torture. I beg you.

Jesus: It is finished. *(Candle 7 is extinguished.)*

Mary: It is finished. *(Mary blows out the Christ candle and exits. The sanctuary should be dark, at least for a period of time.)*

The service closes with a hymn, prayer, benediction, or complete silence in the darkened sanctuary.

Appendix A

SUGGESTED PREPARATION EXERCISES AND TECHNIQUES

TOTAL BODY EXERCISES FOR LOOSENING AND STRETCHING

UPPER BODY

1. Turn head as far as you can comfortably to the right and then the left. Hold for 5 counts.
2. Swing head slowly each direction, a total of 6 times.
3. Roll shoulders backward 10 times and forward 10.
4. Extend right arm straight up, bend at the elbow and reach behind head, trying to touch the upper back. Grasp the arm at the elbow with your left hand and hold for 10. Repeat on the other side.
5. Clasp hands behind you with arms straight and hold for 10. Repeat in front, hold 10.
6. Extend arms straight out from sides and circle, slow and big, 5 one direction, and 5 in the opposite direction.
7. Circle each wrist, 5 times each direction.
8. Step forward on right foot with weight on the forward foot, bend that knee, and reach with right arm above head, feeling the stretch in the right side. Repeat on the other side.
9. With legs apart, bend at the waist as far as is comfortable, keeping legs and back straight. Hold 5. Repeat over left leg, then over right.
10. Standing on one foot, circle each ankle as you did with the wrists, 5 each direction. If necessary, hold on to

something to maintain balance, but attempt to do this without holding on because the exercise improves balance.

11. Bend the right leg behind you, grasp foot and hold near buttocks for 10. Repeat with left leg.

12. Bend left knee. Extend right leg behind you, toes pointed forward, pressing heel into floor. Place hands on left thigh, keeping back and right leg straight. Hold 10. Repeat with left leg.

FLOOR EXERCISES, OPTIONAL, GOOD FOR BACK.

13. Lie on back, knees up, feet on floor; raise right knee as close to chest as possible, hold with hands and exert a little pressure. Hold 5. Repeat with left knee. Do 5 on each side.

14. Repeat the above exercise with both knees together, holding 15. With knees bent and feet on floor, slowly swivel knees to the right, trying to keep left shoulder on the floor. Hold 5. Repeat on the left.

15. With knees bent and feet on floor, raise head and shoulders from floor, a few inches and hold 5. Repeat 10 times.

16. With knees bent, feet on floor, extend the right leg as straight up as possible and hold 5. Repeat with the left leg.

VOCAL EXERCISES

SOME TECHNIQUES FOR SPEECH

A Vocabulary: tempo—fast/slow
pitch—high/low
intensity—light/harsh/through gritted teeth.
volume—loud/soft
quality—aristocratic, ordinary, uneducated, accented.

OVERLAPPING ARGUMENT TECHNIQUE

The words of the argument are not as important as the fact of the argument and the feelings it engenders in listeners. The following dialogue is an imaginary dialogue adapted from Matthew 18:28-30, the parable of forgiveness. This is good practice for varying speech patterns and tone. Begin allowing each person to speak his or her full lines; but as the argument moves along, increase the tempo, pitch, intensity, and volume until the speakers are interrupting each other's lines the way we do when we are angry.

Servant A: It's time to pay back the money you owe me.

Servant B: I don't have it, but I will if you give me a little more time.

Servant A: The agreement was for you to pay the money on this date.

Servant B: Give me until the first of the month. Please.

Servant A: No, I want it now.

Servant B: Shouldn't you show me the same kindness the master showed you?

Servant A: That's none of your business. Let's have it.

Servant B: I said I can't give it to you now.

Servant A: Then you will go to jail.

Servant B: That's not fair.

Servant A: No, it's not fair; it's life.

Some of the best exercises are those that have been around for a long time: Recite each of the following, having someone else listen and evaluate your pronunciation. While speed is usually the goal of children when playing with these words, your goal is clarity and precision.

1. How now brown cow.
2. Rubber baby buggy bumper.
3. Sally sells seashells down by the seashore.
4. The skunk sat on the stump. The skunk said the stump stunk. The stump said the skunk stunk. Which do you think stunk? The skunk or the stump.

Repeat the following sentences, emphasizing a different word each time. All but *to* should be emphasized. Concentrate not only on the different inflections, but also on enunciating *t*'s so that *want you* does not sound like *wanchew*.

I don't want you to go.

You will come with me.

Read a scripture passage expressing a different emotion each time.

CLOWNING EXERCISES

Loosen up your body with the exercises that follow.

1. Exercise your face by distorting your mouth and squeezing features together. Squint into an imaginary sun. Open your eyes wide in surprise. Holding your head still, look to the left, then to the right.

2. Play pass the face. Sit in a circle. First person turns with back to everybody and creates a distorted facial expression. The person next to him mirrors it and passes it along to the next and so on.[1]

3. Express the following feelings with your face and body and without sound. Let others watch and suggest ways to make expressions more clear. When finished, each person selects only one of the feelings and expresses it to the group, allowing them to guess which feeling it is.

   Anxiety, real fear, terror.

   Peacefulness, happiness, joy.

   Annoyance, aggravation, anger

   Boredom by degrees.

1. Floyd Shaffer and Penne Sewall, *Clown Ministry* (Loveland, Colo.: Group Books, 1984), 28.

CENTERING EXERCISE

1. Close your eyes and take a deep, slow breath, breathing from the abdomen, not the chest. Count to 6 as you fill your lungs. Hold for a second, and slowly exhale. Repeat 4 times. As you do this, think: "This is the breath of air God has given me today."
2. From the top of your head to the tip of your toes, visualize the miracle of your body.
3. Smooth out the frown wrinkles on your forehead, relax the muscles in your face, jaw, and neck. Feel tension slide from your shoulders, down your arms, through your hands, out the finger tips. Start at the base of your skull and work the tension down your spine and out the tailbone. Feel yourself untie the knots in your abdomen. Visualize healthy internal organs one by one: your heart, stomach, liver, gall bladder (if you have one), lungs. Thank God for this amazing machine. Relax the muscles in your thighs and calves, feeling the strength and power in your legs. Even legs that don't function as well as they once did may still hold you up. Ease the tension from your feet. Marvel at the miracle of feet.
4. Look inside yourself at what is not tangible—the spirit or the soul of you. What does it look and feel like? What music is in your soul? Forget your body and lose yourself in your soul.
5. Meet Jesus now. Let him take your hand, touch your hair, smile at you, hug you. Let him look any way you think he would look. Allow him to come to you as a real person but one with great wisdom. Talk to him. Hear him. Relax in his presence for a while.
6. Say good-bye to Jesus, withdraw slowly from your inner space. Come back with body, mind, and spirit refreshed.

CREATING A CLOWN FACE

SUPPLIES NEEDED: Mirror, something to hold your hair back from your face, tissues, cotton swabs, soft cosmetic brush or shaving brush, large fluffy powder puff, sponge or spray bottle, clown white greasepaint, black lining pencil, clown colors or red and black (blue, yellow, green optional), talcum powder, lotion for a base, baby or vegetable oil for removal.

STEPS FOR APPLYING

1. Start with a clean face. Tie hair back, and apply a lotion. Wipe away any excess.
2. With your fingers, apply a thin coat (not so thin your skin shows through) of white over entire face and neck.
3. With a cotton swab or tissue, remove white from the areas you intend to cover with another color, such as the lips, end of your nose, and a round circle on the cheeks.
4. Apply powder over all the white until there are no shiny areas or until it does not feel sticky to the touch. (Hold your breath while powdering.)
5. Wait a couple of minutes, then gently brush off the excess powder with the soft brush.
6. Apply the colors, using a lining stick or your fingers to fill in the spaces. When drawing on your mouth, avoid red makeup above your upper lip.
7. Powder after each color is applied. Powder once more overall.
8. Remove excess powder and set your makeup by applying water or blotting with a wet sponge or spraying from a bottle filled with water or splashing the face with fingers dipped in water.
9. Smile. Check teeth for color. (You don't want any there.) Touch all areas that have been colored to check for stickiness. Powder again if necessary.

RESOURCES AND REFERENCES

Listed below are various publications, organizations, and workshop leaders. Many more resources are available and can often be found through local libraries and bookstores.

REFERENCES WITHIN TEXT

Berthier, Jacques. 1984. *Laudate:* Music of Taizé. Dublin, Ireland: Veritas Productions Audio.

Harper's Bible Dictionary. 1973. New York: Harper&Row.

Hopkins, Mary Rice. 1990. "Easter Rise Up." In *Come, Meet Jesus.* Boston: St. Paul Books and Media. Cassette produced by Denny Bouchard, Daughters of St. Paul, 50 St. Paul's Ave., Boston, MA 02130.

Hopkins, Mary Rice. 1990. "Easter Rise Up." In *Come, Meet Jesus: Children's Music by Mary Rice Hopkins.* Boston: St. Paul Books.

Reader's Digest Association. 1974. *Great People of the Bible and How They Lived.* Pleasantville, NY: Reader's Digest Association.

Reader's Digest Association. 1987. *Jesus and His Times.* Pleasantville, NY: Reader's Digest Association.

Shaffer, Floyd and Penne Sewall. 1984. *Clown Ministry,* Loveland, Colo.: Group Books.
   Includes makeup and specific ideas for clown exercises, Group Books, Box 481, Loveland, CO 80539.

EPIGRAPHS

Foreword: Angelou, Maya. 1997. *Even the Stars Look Lonesome.* New York: Random House, 133.

Introduction: Whiting, Karen H. 1998. *Upper Room.* Edited by Stephen D. Bryant. Nashville: Upper Room Books (May-June).

Chapter 1: Brown, Les. Quoted in Julia Cameron. 1992. *The Artist's Way.* G. P. Putnam's Sons: New York, 123.

Chapter 2: Weems, Ann. 1980. *Reaching for Rainbows.* Philadelphia: Westminster Press, 12.

Chapter 5: Jacques, Susan. 1992. Pastor, Lemont United Methodist Church, 25 West Custer, Lemont, Illinois.

RESOURCES

RELIGIOUS PUBLISHERS OF CATALOGUES FOR DRAMA, SACRED DANCE, AND CLOWNING

Abingdon Press, 201 Eighth Avenue, P.O. Box 801, Nashville, TN 37202-0801 (615) 749-6303, Fax (615) 749-6512.

Church Growth Institute, P.O. Box 7000, Forest, VA 24551, (804) 525-0022, Fax (804) 525-0608.

Contemporary Drama, Box 7710, Colorado Springs, CO 80933.

Eldridge Publishing Co., P.O. Box 1595, Venice, FL 34184, 1-800-95-CHURCH, Fax 1-800-453-5179.

The Sharing Company, P.O. Box 2224, Austin, TX 78768-2224.

BOOKS THAT NURTURE YOUR CREATIVITY

Cameron, Julia. 1992. *The Artist's Way.* New York: G. P. Putnam's Sons. Offers courage.

Weems, Ann. 1980. *Reaching for Rainbows.* Philadelphia: The

Westminster Press. Stimulates creativity and provides skits and skit ideas.

RESOURCES FOR DRAMA AND SCRIPTURE

Bradford, Grace. 1995. *Scriptures Come Alive.* Nashville: Abingdon Press.

Boomershine, Thomas. 1988. *Story Journey: An Invitation to the Gospel as Storytelling.* Nashville: Abingdon Press.

Dewey, Dennis, Audiotapes include "The Light and the Life: Stories from the Gospel of John"; "The Stories of Christmas"; and "A Celebration of the Senses."

Videotapes include "In the Beginning, Toward the Middle, All the Way to the End"; "It Is Finished"; "How to Tell and Learn a Bible Story"; and "That You May Believe." Network of Bible Storytellers: 1810 Harvard Blvd., Dayton, OH 45406.

Flinn, Lisa and Younger, Barbara. 1993. *Creative Ways to Offer Praise.* Nashville: Abingdon Press.

Goens, Linda M. *Easter Season* and *Pilgrim Women,* available from Eldridge Plays and Musicals, P.O. Box 1595, Venice, FL 34284.

_____*I Wait . . . I Wonder* and *My Son the Messiah,* available from Contemporary Drama, 885 Elkton Drive, Colorado Springs, CO 80907.

_____*Resurrection on Trial,* previously published by Contemporary Drama, appearing as part of an Easter anthology (forthcoming, 1999).

MacDonald, Margaret Read. 1993. *The Storyteller's Start-Up Book.* Little Rock: August House.

Rucker, Robert M. 1993. *Producing and Directing Drama for the Church.* Kansas City, Mo.: Lillenas Publishing.

RESOURCES FOR DANCE

Costello, Elaine. 1986. *Religious Signing.* New York: Bantam Books.

De Sola, Carla. 1986. *The Spirit Moves*. Austin, Texas: The Sharing Company.

Riekehof, Lottie L. 1987. *The Joy of Signing*, 2nd ed. Springfield, MS: Gospel Publishing House.

Taylor, Margaret, with sketches by Sally Sargent Turner. 1980. *Look Up and Live*. Austin: The Sharing Company.

RESOURCES FOR CLOWNING

Litherland, Janet. 1982. *The Clown Ministry Handbook*. Colorado Springs: Meriwether Publishing.

Toomey, Susan K. 1986. *Mime Ministry*. Colorado Springs: Meriwether Publishing.

WORKSHOP LEADERS FOR DANCE

Mary Bell, 6108 Regina Circle, Indianapolis, IN 46224.

Therese Chatelaine, Director Jubilate Liturgical Dance, 6649 Shore Island Drive, Indianapolis, IN 46220; (317) 259-7136.

Kara Miller Esposito, Director of the Omega Dance Company, Cathedral of St. John the Divine, 1047 Amsterdam, New York, NY 10024; (212) 666-0256.

Carolyn Greene, Director and Choreographer of SON-DANCE Sacred Dance Ministry, First United Methodist Church, 336 S. Halifax Dr., Ormond Beach, FL 32176; (904) 615-4832 or (904) 677-1442.

WORKSHOP LEADERS FOR SCRIPTURE INTERPRETATION AND STORYTELLING

Grace Bradford, Dramatic Scripture Interpretation, 641 Ingraham Street, NW, Washington, D.C. 20011; (202) 882-5137.

Dennis Dewey, Storytelling, www.DennisDewey.org, (1-800-STORY-XL) (1-800-786-7995); or visit www.nobs.org.

WORKSHOP LEADER FOR CREATIVE ARTS IN WORSHIP AND SPIRITUAL JOURNALING

Linda M. Goens, 147 Park Lane, Carmel, IN, 46032; (317) 846-3279 or at Church of the Saviour, 5400 East 62nd Street, Indianapolis, IN, 46220; (317) 251-6187.

ORGANIZATIONS

American Dance Guild, 31 West 21st Street, 3rd floor, New York, NY 10010; (212) 627-3790.

The Fellowship of United Methodists in Music and Worship Arts, P.O. Box 24787, Nashville, TN 37202; (615) 749-6875.

Fellowship of Merry Christians, P.O. Box 668, Kalamazoo, MI 490005.

NOBS, Network of Biblical Storytellers, 1810 Harvard Blvd., Dayton, OH 45406; 1-800-355-NOBS.

Sacred Dance Guild, 1004 Brook Ridge Circle SE, Huntsville, AL 35801; (205) 881-8171 or Fax (205) 880-8628.

SCRIPTURE INDEX

Psalm 27:1. 91
  movement
Psalm 34:18 53
  contemporary drama skit
Psalm 51:17 53
  contemporary drama skit
Psalm 104:31-35. 94
  movement
Psalm 119:105 91
  movement

Proverbs 3:17 139
  clown skit
Proverbs 11:12 134
  clown skit
Proverbs 22:6. 51
  contemporary drama skit
Proverbs 22:10. 53
  contemporary drama skit

Isaiah 11:1-10. . . . . . . 152, 168
  drama service
Isaiah 60:20 91
  movement

Matthew 1:18-25 . . . . . 152, 157
  drama skit
Matthew 2:1-12. 59
  contemporary drama skit
  reading 63
Matthew 5:5 128
  clown skit
Matthew 5:16 91
  movement
Matthew 5:44 134
  clown skit
Matthew 6:19-21 145
  clown skit

Matthew 7:1 134
  clown skit
Matthew 7:9-12. 51
  contemporary drama skit
Matthew 11:18 53
  contemporary drama skit
Matthew 13:1-23. 141
  clown skit
Matthew 19:13-14. 51
  contemporary drama skit
Matthew 20:26-27 128
  clown skit
Matthew 23. 64
  drama and movement
Matthew 25:31-40. 49
  contemporary drama skit
Matthew 25:34-36. 139
  clown skit
Matthew 26:31-35. 173
  drama service
Matthew 26:57–27:37 177
  drama service
Matthew 27:11-55. 106
  movement
Matthew 27:27-31. 100
  movement
Matthew 28:16-20. 37
  choral scripture reading

Mark 2:1-12. 45
  scripture skit
Mark 4:3-8, 14-20 141
  clown skit
Mark 12:37b-44 148
  clown skit
Mark 15:1-40 106
  movement

Mark 15:16-20 100
    movement
Mark 15:33-34 177
    drama service

Luke 1:5-38 . . . . 151, 154
    drama skit
Luke 1:26-38 96
    movement
Luke 1:39-56 . . . . 152, 159
    movement
Luke 2:1-20 . . . . 152, 168
    drama service
Luke 2:8-14 . . . . 152, 161
    drama, music
Luke 8:4-15 141
    clown skit
Luke 22:41-45 173
    drama service
Luke 22:66–23:49 106
    movement
Luke 23:32-34, 36-46 177
    drama service
Luke 24:1-8 110
    movement

John 1:4 91
    movement
John 4:10-26 57
    scripture skit
John 8:12 91
    movement
John 10:1-18 42
    scripture as story
John 12:13 64
    drama and movement
John 12:36 91
    movement
John 13:1-10, 12-17, 37-38 . . . 173
    drama service

John 15:1-6, 9-12 40
    choral scripture reading
John 18:28-40 106
    movement
John 19:25-30 177
    drama service
John 19:28-30 106
    movement

Acts 2:1-8, 14-38 114
    movement

1 Corinthians 12 128
    clown skit

Galatians 5:13 128
    clown skit

Ephesians 5:8 90
    movement

Philippians 2:3 128
    clown skit

Colossians 3:12-14 134
    clown skit

James 2:14-18 139
    clown skit

1 John 1:5 91
    movement
1 John 1:7 91
    movement
1 John 3:17-18 139
    clown skit
1 John 3:18-20 53
    contemporary drama skit